THE BIOGRAPHY OF
MARIO BALOTELLI,
CITY'S LEGENDARY
STRIKER

WHY ALWAYS ME?

FRANK WORRALL

JB

JOHN BLAKE

Published by John Blake Publishing Ltd,
3 Bramber Court, 2 Bramber Road,
London W14 9PB, England

www.johnblakepublishing.co.uk

www.facebook.com/Johnblakepub facebook
twitter.com/johnblakepub twitter

First published in hardback in 2013

ISBN: 978-1-78219-017-2

British Library Cataloguing-in-Publication Data:

A catalogue record for this book is available from the British Library.

Design by www.envydesign.co.uk

Printed in Great Britain by CPI Group (UK) Ltd, Croydon, CR0 4YY

1 3 5 7 9 10 8 6 4 2

Papers used by John Blake Publishing are natural, recyclable products
made from wood grown in sustainable forests. The manufacturing processes
conform to the environmental regulations of the country of origin.

Every attempt has been made to contact the relevant copyright-holders,
but some were unobtainable. We would be grateful if the
appropriate people could contact us.

This book is dedicated to the following:

IN ENGLAND – Loyal Manchester City fans Craig Bodell and Caroline Sterling, and journalist Howard Cooper of the *Sun*.

IN ITALY – Journalist Nick Pisa, to whom I am indebted for providing all the background and early life material on Mario from birth to 15, particularly for Nick's interviews with the family, close friends and associates of the footballer back in Italy.

The initial profits I make from this book are funding my 14-year-old son Frankie's humanitarian trip to Uganda to help underprivileged orphans by teaching in schools, helping to grow crops and building facilities in the local area – causes I know are close to Mario Balotelli's heart.

For more details on Frank Worrall and his books see www.frankworrall.com

CONTENTS

ACKNOWLEDGEMENTS

Special thanks: Nick Pisa in Rome, John Blake, Allie Collins and all at John Blake Publishing. Alan Feltham and the boys at *SunSport*, and Dominic Turnbull.

THANKS: Gary Edwards, Adrian Baker, Ben Felsenburg, Alex Butler, Danny Bottono, Steven Gordon, Lee Clayton, BBC Sport, Dave Morgan, Darren O'Driscoll, David and Nicki Burgess, Pravina Patel, Martin Creasy, Lee Hassall, Ian Rondeau, Colin Forshaw, John Fitzpatrick, Roy Stone, Russell Forgham and Tom Henderson Smith.

Not forgetting: Angela, Frankie, Jude, Nat, Barbara, Frank, Bob and Stephen, Gill, Lucy, Alex, Suzanne, Michael and William.

'Balotelli is the greatest living human being ever. He is not of this world. If he played for any other club, we'd still love him.'

Rocker and Manchester City fanatic
Noel Gallagher on his favourite footballer.

CHAPTER ONE

A TROUBLED BOY

His childhood certainly was no easy ride. He would suffer from health problems and poverty – and would eventually end up living with foster parents. His troubled childhood would be a key factor in moulding his character and the person he would become as a footballer and would certainly contribute to the insecurities, defensiveness and pained psyche that would plague him as he became an international star.

Mario Barwuah Balotelli was born on August 12, 1990, in Palermo, Sicily, to Ghanaian immigrants Thomas and Rose Barwuah. They were poor and Mario lived in cramped accommodation with his parents and his sister Abigail, three years his elder. Thomas proved he would graft for his family by travelling back and forth every weekend on a 12-hour overnight train to find manual work, many miles away from their home. Rose stayed at home to look after Mario and Abigail. But Rose and Thomas faced further problems as Mario was in and out of hospital for the first two years of his life. He was diagnosed with life-threatening complications to his intestines shortly after birth, and would need a series of operations.

Thomas said, 'There were complications with Mario's intestines and he was in a bad way. The doctors were worried that he would not survive and we even had him baptised in hospital in case he died. For a year we were frantic with worry that he would not live. He was our first-born son and we were so proud when he was born, but we were left facing the prospect he might die.'

But Mario was a born fighter and by the age of two his condition had improved dramatically. The family now moved to Bagnolo on the outskirts of Brescia in northern Italy. They were still poor and initially lived in a cramped studio flat with another African family before asking social services for help, pointing out Mario had recently recovered from an operation.

Social services officers sympathised with their plight – and suggested that it might be for the best if Mario moved in with foster parents. The officers thought Mario would benefit if he went to live with Francesco and Silvio Balotelli, a white couple who already had two sons and a daughter of their own. Francesco, a warehouse supervisor in the pasta trade (now retired) and Silvio, originally a nurse and then a foster mother through much of her married life, lived in a big house in Concesio, an affluent nearby town, and social services pointed out to the Barwuahs that the move would bring stability and comfort to their son, who had suffered so much with his failing health.

Thomas Barwuah said: 'At first we were not sure but we

decided it was probably best for Mario. We saw him every week and we all got on really well.'

Soon the Barwuahs moved to a council flat above a row of shops – and, two years after Mario was born, had another son, Enoch, who would also become a professional footballer. Thomas said he and his wife had agreed to a one-year foster placement, which was then extended by a further 12 months. But a division was opening up which would prove impossible to heal.

Thomas said, 'We thought that at some point, once things had sorted out, Mario would come back to us. But instead, every time we tried to get him back, the Balotellis kept extending the foster time. We couldn't afford lawyers to fight for us, so Mario grew more and more distant.

'He would come and visit and play with his brothers and sisters but he just didn't seem to have any time for us, his mother and father. We wanted him back for more than 10 years but, every time we tried, the courts blocked it.'

Instead Mario was brought up by the Balotellis. Even inside a well-off family he suffered at times – being the black child of white parents. It would lead him to turning his back on his Ghanaian heritage, taking the surname of his adopted parents and eventually becoming an Italian national. Inevitably, he would suffer racial abuse at school and in the street as he grew up with the Balotellis and would become 'both introverted and combustible' according to those who witnessed his development. His foster mother Silvio Balotelli would later outline his particular difficulties when she said, 'He was born and raised in Italy but had to suffer the humiliation and hardships of being considered a foreigner.'

I asked a psychotherapist friend to comment on Mario's

situation. She said, 'It is not hard to see that he would have problems growing up. He must have suffered a sort of double identity crisis. On the one hand, he didn't know who were his real parents and would feel confusion and maybe guilt at choosing one over the other. Plus there would be anger at his biological parents for giving him away.

'Then you have the scenario of a black boy growing up in a white family. That must have also been confusing for him and he would surely get angry and defensive at being racially abused by other kids – although I am sure his new family would be loving and supportive. It all points to a young man with problems underneath the surface – anger, resentment, confusion and sadness – and all it would take would be something surrounding his situation for those simmering problems to boil over. I would imagine he could fly off the handle very easily. He might ultimately need therapy to "bring closure" to his upbringing and to help him cope emotionally with life. He might need cognitive help to bring his temper under control and to put a lid on those demons.'

At this stage, I must declare my indebtedness to Nick Pisa, the British journalist who operates for the UK press from Italy. Pisa has delved beneath the surface to uncover the problems Mario faced as a youngster – and all the quotes in this chapter are included courtesy of him. Pisa learned at first hand in Italy of the tug-of-war between the Barwuahs and the Balotellis that would lead to a breakdown of relations between Mario and his birth family.

Pisa says, 'According to Mario he was abandoned by his parents in hospital when he was two years old. It's a claim Thomas and Rose deny adamantly.

'I tracked down Thomas and Rose to their third floor

council flat at Bagnolo Mella, where they live with their three other children Abigail, 22, Enoch, 17, and Angel, 11.

'Both Thomas and Rose have remained in the shadows ever since Mario hit the big time when he made his debut for Inter Milan at just 17 years old – after being turned down by Spanish giants Barcelona. Metal worker Thomas was close to tears as he proudly showed me pictures of young Mario as a baby and toddler growing up in the Sicilian city of Palermo before they moved north to Brescia.'

Pisa says Thomas and Rose were stunned when they learned that Mario had claimed they had let him down – Thomas told Nick, 'Mario was convinced we had abandoned him in a hospital but that's not true.' They were further shocked when Mario was reported to have said, "My real parents only want to know me now I am famous".'

Thomas told Pisa, 'I'm so fed up with Mario. How can he say we just want to know him for his money – it's not true – we gave him all the love we could.

'We have never spoken out because we didn't want to ruin his career but now enough is enough. I am fed up with Mario saying we abandoned him and I am fed up with him saying we just want his money.'

Pisa says, 'Certainly photographs dotted around the house are testimony of what appears to have been a happy normal childhood – Mario playing football, Mario in a suit at a family function, Mario play fighting his brother as Rose looks on. Thomas showed another photograph of Mario holding a football standing next to a three-year-old friend and said: "That picture was taken after he had spent hours playing football in the rain. We were at a friend's house in Vicenza and when the boys came in they were soaked but they were laughing and joking despite being wet and my friend said to Mario, "You really are Super Mario" and it's the name we gave him.'

Thomas added, 'You can see why we loved him and we still love him now, that's why I get so angry when I hear he's said these things about us. We don't want any money. We are Christians and every morning I thank God that I have my legs, my arms, my body and that I can work and provide for my family. We are not bothered about money because the more money you have then you lose respect for God. I'm happy with what I have and don't want anything, I just want us to get on.'

Thomas also said that during Mario's four years at Inter his son had only invited him to watch him play once and that was when they played Chelsea in the Champions League.

Thomas said: 'He turned up one day with four tickets and he gave them to his brother – I asked if I could come and watch and he said that Enoch had the tickets and he could do what he wanted with them. I don't want anything from him. I just want us to get on – now he is going to England and he will become even more famous. I don't think I will go there to see him – maybe his brother or his sisters will go but we won't go. He is not the same boy I knew when he was younger always laughing and smiling, he was trouble but in a good way.'

Thomas also described to Nick Pisa how he and his wife were not even invited to the ceremony when Mario was made an Italian citizen on his 18th birthday, saying: 'We didn't know anything about that until we saw it on the news. I didn't even know that he had taken the surname Balotelli. I thought he would still have our surname but he chose not to take it – I wish I knew why he is treating us like this.'

Thomas added, 'I saw him earlier this month and he told us that he would be moving to Manchester and like any father would I wish him well. I was so proud when he joined Inter and I am still proud of him I just want us to be how we were.'

Nick Pisa would later also uncover a split between Mario and his big sister, Abigail Barwuah. She would add to her father's criticisms, saying he had failed to keep in touch with his natural family over the years. Abigail added that he was risking his career after a series of high-profile incidents at City and she would echo the pleas of City manager Roberto Mancini and the Italian national coach Cesare Prandelli that her brother should 'take it easy' or risk 'throwing his career away.'

Abigail had become angry after she claimed Mario had shunned her as well as his parents. A month earlier, she had been voted off Italy's version of *I'm A Celebrity: Get Me Out of Here!* and she slammed her brother for not taking part in studio calls from Rome to the island off Honduras where the reality show was taking place.

She stormed: 'My brother has really disappointed me. It's clear to me that I don't mean anything to him. He didn't come into the studio, he didn't make a phone call and even his family haven't seen him. He is very self centred, maybe he doesn't want me to use him but I can make it on my own. I'm glad that I have shown I am not like him.

'He needs to try and calm down. I can't justify his behaviour anymore. He is nearly 21 years old and he is putting his career at risk.'

Abigail said: 'I was away for six weeks with the show and I never heard a word from him – when I speak about my siblings I'm talking only about Enoch and Angel. After being on *I'm A Celebrity* I realised that Mario didn't care about me. He could have come into the studio, just once to give me some support, even just a telephone call. He didn't do it during the show and he didn't do it afterwards – I haven't heard a thing from him. In six weeks that I was away he didn't even call to ask how I was, he didn't even call to see how his family were and Angel doesn't want to see him. Maybe he is annoyed that someone else in the family is famous. I've asked myself why he is like he is but I can't find an answer. Mario has never bothered to help me, even when he became famous and I don't mean financially. I have never been bothered about his money.'

Abigail then added: 'In the past when he was having a rough time I was there for him. I was there for him when everyone attacked him but now he is certainly not going to get any help from me any more. I'm sorry for what's happened to him but now he has to grow up. He is nearly 21 years old and he needs to start thinking. He cannot carry on with his Balotelli escapades – it's one thing to do them when you are 18 but it's another thing doing them now. It's time he calmed down otherwise he is really putting his career at risk. I'm glad that by taking part in *I'm A Celebrity* I've proved that our family is educated and I am not liking him.'

When asked if she would like to see her brother again Abigail said: 'I don't want to see him now. He has really disappointed me. He doesn't deserve my love and he doesn't deserve to be considered a brother.'

The Balotellis have always maintained a dignified silence on the matter. And while they have not commented on the claims of the Barwuahs, Mario himself has issued an official statement on the matter, saying, 'I had already asked my birth parents to respect my privacy, just as my family always has done, but they didn't listen to me. I have no other recourse than to repeat what I said two years ago: if I hadn't become the football star Mario Balotelli, they wouldn't have cared what happened to me. My birth parents have said some incorrect and vague things which put my adoptive family in a bad light. This is something I cannot let pass, especially because my real family lives in Brescia – the family that has always loved and raised me. They are the only family who really know me as Mario. Perhaps in Brescia they don't know that I stayed with my family uninterrupted for 16 years, the foster situation renewed every couple of years by the tribunal. Maybe they don't know that I personally asked for adoption since the age of 13, but only managed to make it official in December 2008.'

While Mario may, as a youngster, have had struggled with identity problems and keeping his footing in an Italian society that was at the time bedevilled by racist attitude, he had no problem keeping his footing on the football pitch – or in the garden or the local park as he developed into a fine young player. His foster father Franco played a big part in his development – taking time out to drive Mario to football practice, football matches plus all the other activities Mario, as a busy boy who loved sport, liked to partake in. They included being in the Scouts, playing basketball, running with the local athletics club, swimming and martial arts. Mario particularly loved karate and judo and it is often said that he would maybe have gone down the road of choosing martial arts as an alternative career had football not proved his saving grace.

He may not have been the most academically gifted boy in the class, but he was certainly the best athlete and the best footballer. On his personal website, www.mariobalotelli.it, Mario outlines how much he owes to the Balotellis for their love, comfort and encouragement – and how he himself knew he had a talent at football, 'Mario was born in Palermo on 12 August 1990, but has lived in Brescia with the Balotelli family since he was two. From the very start mum, dad, brothers Corrado and Giovanni, and sister Cristina (all much older than him) looked after little Mario with all the love of a parent, brother or sister. When he was just five Mario began playing football for the Mompiano parish team and was immediately grouped with the older boys because of his exceptional technical skills.'

Balotelli was on the road that would lead to superstardom – and to him becoming one of the world's most famous footballers. But his foster mother Silvio was not convinced he was on the right track and urged him to spend more time on his studies...or even to consider becoming a basketball player! Giovanni Valenti, now youth team coach at AC Milan, told how he used to train Mario at Mompiano as a kid – and had to persuade Silvio that his future should be in football. Valenti said, 'His mother was not keen on the idea of him having a career in football. When he started having trials at decent local clubs, she made him recite his multiplication tables, like usual, while all the other parents were taking in advice.

'One time she even tried to stop him playing football and make him take up basketball. I jumped up and protested because that would have been a terrible waste. He was much better than his contemporaries – and still is.'

Even at the age of five, at Mompiano, he would also suffer racial discrimination as he played football. Mauro Tomolini, who ran the Mompiano team, said parents of other children tried to get him out of the team. Tomolini said, 'When he came here aged five, he was the only black child out of 250. The parents of the others looked at him differently. People asked us to get him out of the team.' Is it any wonder that Mario grew up defensive and suspicious of people and their motives - when he was verbally abused for the colour of his skin at such a young age?

It was disgraceful and a sad comment on Italian society at that time and the problem for Mario was that even in his late teens he would still suffer abuse from the terraces when he turned out for Inter Milan. In 2009 would come the worst of it – when he was first abused by Roma fans and then, on a much worse scale, by fans of Juventus. Balotelli had scored in the 1-1 draw at Juventus in April of that year, and the *Guardian*'s Paolo Bandini summed up the unacceptable nature of the chanting that day, 'During the match the Internazionale striker Mario Balotelli had been subjected to a stream of racist taunts and chants. "If I had been in the stadium, after a certain point I would have left my seat in the stands, I would have gone down on to the pitch and taken my team out of the game," said Internazionale's president, Massimo Moratti.

'Juventus can expect to receive a fine, though it is unlikely to put a significant dent in their finances. Roma were forced to pay just €8,000 (£7,100) when their fans directed similar abuse at Balotelli during their 3–3 draw in March, on condition that they took steps to prevent any repeat. The Juventus president, Giovanni Cobolli Gigli, has condemned the chanting and will doubtless hope to receive similar terms.

'Balotelli, for his part, will feel that he answered the abuse in the best possible way. It was his team-mate Zlatan Ibrahimovic who once responded to the jeers of Juventus fans by insisting that "they will only make me stronger" but, while the Swede is yet to score against his former club, Balotelli's strike on Saturday was his third in as many appearances against the Bianconeri.'

After the match, Mario stood proud against his abusers, merely saying, 'I am more Italian than those Juventus fans in the stands.'

Later Mario would expand upon how he suffered as a child because he was black. He would say, 'Two things were close to my heart as a boy. Like all boys of a certain age, I was interested in girls and getting attention. But it was like I was transparent [invisible]. I'm no George Clooney but I couldn't explain why I was ignored. My friends in Italy explained. They told me people don't like blacks.'

Juventus would eventually be forced to play one of their matches behind closed doors because of fans' abuse of him and it would only be when he came to England that the catcalls would end – and that would be one of the key factors in his decision not to rush back to Italy at the end of his first season, when he was homesick for his family and friends. He knew he was in a fairer, more multicultural society in England than Italy and that decided it for him: he would stay put in Manchester.

Back in his childhood, his next move, aged eight or nine, on the road to the top was to San Bartolomeo, a youth team in a nearby town. Mario again made his mark, he was growing physically now and was not as easily knocked off the ball. And when he was pushed aside he would react angrily and push back: the first signs of the famous Balotelli temper were beginning to surface. It would become even more apparent when he reached the age of 11 and signed for the Italian Serie C outfit AC Lumezzane. Even at that tender age, Mario knew what he wanted and what he would accept – and what he would not accept. His first major brush with authority came when he told the club's coach, Giovanni Valenti – the man who had been so influential in his development at Mompiano and who had now moved on to Lumezzane as youth coach – that he would not play under his surname of Barwuah.

Valenti said: 'We had to make alterations on the team sheet and ask the stadium announcer not to call him Barwuah, but Balotelli. If he refused, we had to beg him to use just his first name. Otherwise, Mario wouldn't play.'

And his team-mate Marco Pedretti added, 'We used to fight in the dressing room. I threw him against a radiator once because he had hidden my clothes and I was stood there in my underpants like an idiot. I hadn't seen him for a good while when he called me a few years ago from Inter Milan. It was his birthday and he asked me if I wanted to spend it with him. He never had many friends.'

In 2005, at the age of 15, Mario caught the eye of Lumezzane's first team coach Walter Salvioni, who knew immediately that he had a raw diamond on his hands. Salvioni took Mario under his wing and into the Italian third division club's senior squad. Salvioni said, 'I was watching the juniors train and saw Mario on the pitch – after just five minutes I knew I had to have him in the first squad. He was incredible. His touch was fantastic. I went to the junior coach and said, "I'm taking that lad for the first team". I didn't know he was only 15 until the coach said, "You can't, he's too young".'

The club's chairman and the league decided Balotelli could play if Lumezzane got a doctor's certificate to say he was fit enough to appear at senior level. 'Within 24 hours he was with us,' said Salvioni. 'He spent a day training with the first team and then he was on the coach with us for the match in Genoa. They were up near the top and we were third from bottom, but we ended up winning 1-0. Mario came on for the last 30 minutes and won the corner from which we scored the winner.'

It was a brave gamble by the coach although Salvioni is quick to deny that there was any risk involved. 'He was a natural, I knew he had what it took to make it from that first day when I saw him', he said. 'Mario is an all-round talented player. He can beat his opponents for pace and skill and he is very physical. The few months he was with me, I was very impressed with him.'

But even Salvioni could sometimes end up angry at the boy. 'He was always rushing away after training and wouldn't stay for any tactics,' he said. 'I confronted him. He smiled and said, "I have to go home to study". In the end, he confessed he was going to play five-a-side with his friends. He was arrogant even then, but basically he just wanted to play football.'

Indeed he did, and at a higher level than Serie C. His main aim was to play in Serie A – Italy's top-flight league – but he was impatient. He was making his mark and making a name for himself at Lumezzane but it was a slow process. So in

2006, he went for a trial at the Nou Camp, the home of Spanish giants Barcelona. The Barcelona sports newspaper, Sport, says the trial went well and that Mario came very close to earning a permanent deal. He played three matches with the Barca B Cadet team, scoring eight goals and impressed the coaches at the club.

But, according to Sport, his agent wanted Mario to earn more money than Barca wanted to splash out ('far from the average figure for a player of his age'), so Mario returned to Italy and Serie C with Lummezane. Later Mario was quoted as jokingly saying, 'I had a trial at Barcelona once, they couldn't handle me. Didn't want me to upstage some guy, Lionel something.'

But he wasn't back at Lummezane for long – his dream of playing in Serie A was imminent. A year after his trial with Barca, Milan giants Internazionale signed him as a 17-year-old. The man who brought him to the San Siro? Roberto Mancini...the partnership between mentor and pupil was about to begin. Mario Balotelli was heading for the bright lights of Milan – and one of the world's biggest, most legendary football clubs.

CHAPTER TWO

INTER THE BIG TIME

He was still 15 when he joined Inter Milan on loan from Lumezzane – and it was a move of considerable impact for a boy of such a tender age. He was moving almost 60 miles away from home and would go straight into Inter's famed youth development programme at the club's training campus.

With other youngsters he would learn about the game from Inter's technical staff and live away in sleeping quarters at the complex. It was a case of having to get over any homesickness and getting on with the job – however painful it may have been.

Luckily, each day would be structured and busy, so the minds of the youngsters were occupied and not drifting off with thoughts of home. Mario settled in well; of course he didn't enjoy being away from home, but he was absolutely determined to make it as a footballer – whatever the personal cost.

He had already come a long way from being adopted to battling through illness and racist issues. He was a tough lad and he was well liked at the Inter training complex. But even at Inter, he could not completely hide his rebellious streak.

If something irked him, the coaches would know. He wasn't a boy who just kept quiet and stayed in the shadows! Inter's junior coach Vincenzo Esposito would recall one particular instance of the famed Balotelli stubbornness. 'The day before an important match we stressed to the players the importance of good preparation,' Esposito said. 'Mario went straight off, bought a huge ice-cream and licked it before my very eyes.' The coaches concede that Mario got away with things that some other kids might not have. He was likeable – and he could score goals. 'It's the old thing of being able to charm and not get a bollocking – basically because you are good at your job,' I was told. 'That was the thing with Mario – he might have been a bit of a rebel at times, but he did the business on the field. You could always rely upon him to pull a goal or two out of the hat just when you needed him to.'

Certainly, making it through the Inter youth programme into the first team squad is no walk in the park. Current Inter youth coach Stefano Bellinzagh recently gave an insight into life at the youth development centre, Interello, where youngsters learn and live.

When asked what characteristics he and the other staff at Interello look for when taking on youngsters, he said, 'During the selection process we first look at three basic main characteristics: technical ability, strength and physical build, and good motor skills. A fourth element and in a way the most important is personality.

'Even at the youth level within a professional club, there are lots of expectations, and young players face a lot of pressures. We choose those players with strong personality traits like leadership and self-confidence, which we think will allow them to deal with pressure situations as they present themselves. Preparation broadens to include game tactics: team systems (man, zone, and mixed zone), and positional play.'

As for Interello itself, it is a dream for a young footballer but could also be a daunting prospect such is the scale, size and ambition of the place. Soccer Magazine Online described it thus, 'Interello is the technical training centre of Inter Milan youth teams. Interello is situated on 30,000 square metres of land and has three regulation grass soccer fields, two earth soccer fields, two seven aside soccer fields, two gyms, two medical rooms, six changing rooms, and sleeping quarters for players living there.'

Mario took it all in his stride when he worked his way up through the youth ranks at the San Siro. Outwardly confident and determined (as they liked to see the youngsters at Interello), he seemed a strong personality. A leader and a star in the making. Of course, the youth coaches did not know the full story – how much he had had to struggle to get there and how that outward strength, some would even call it arrogance even back then, actually masked an inner insecurity and vulnerability.

But the coaches liked what they saw and sensed they had a genius on their hands.

Mario also had the benefit of being spotted by the club's

manager, none other than Roberto Mancini. The boss told his coaches to bring the boy through gently – that he had great potential, but that he would have to be nurtured and encouraged. The big stick would not work with a boy who clearly did not like being dictated to or bullied.

Mario's impact was immediate. He scored goals galore for the juniors and his technique and talent was beyond question. He passed every test and every trial. So it was no surprise when a year later Inter decided he was good enough. When they had initially taken him on loan, they had paid Lumezzane 150,000 euros and now they paid a further 190,000 euros to buy him outright.

He had cost Internazionale a total of 340,000 euros – roughly £230,000. For that they had got a player who would three years later go to Manchester City for a fee of around £23million – not a bad profit and certainly one of the best ever achieved by the Milan outfit.

Not that everyone was pleased by the initial deal that took him from Lumezzane to Milan. The website, theoffside.com, explained in 2008, 'One person who is not on the jovial side [with the final buy-out of Balotelli] is Lumezzane president Renzo Cavagna. Fiorentina and Inter both tried to sign the young phenom, but the Nerazzurri beat out the Viola and added Balotelli to their youth ranks, first on loan, and then signing him on a nominal fee. Balotelli was promoted to the Primavera squad as a 16-year-old, and led Inter to a Scudetto victory. Cavagna is angry because he was not invited to the [victory] ceremony. He also said he has contacted Moratti [Inter chairman] saying that Inter should have given a little more "help" to Lumezzane for the work they did discovering the striker in 2001 and allowing him to grow into the player he is. Moratti never responded to Cavagna – and Cavagna said that they did not even offer his club one Inter Primavera player on loan.'

The war of words did not affect Mario. He now simply got on with the job in hand – namely to ensure that he progressed swiftly and impressively through the youth ranks and on to the first team squad. As long-time Balotelli fan and observer Michael Crigliano explains on YouTube, 'He [Mario] showed his potential in their under-17 squad, known as the Allievi Nazionali, then joined the Primavera under-20 team at the age of 16, quickly becoming a key player.

'He scored a tie-breaking penalty in a Primavera league final 1-0 win over Sampdoria. These performances prompted high praise from several high-ranking people including Inter chairman Massimo Moratti.'

So it was no big surprise that he was fast-tracked to the first team squad. Six months after signing him full-time – and still aged just 17 – Inter decided he was good enough and big enough to withstand the physical and mental rigours of Serie A. Mario had realised his dream. Not only was he in the first team squad, but he had impressed boss Mancini so much that he made his first team debut.

OK, it was only a cameo appearance but it demonstrated the faith that Mancini (and Moratti) had in the boy wonder that he was brought on at all. Mario appeared in the 90th minute of the match at Cagliari with Inter Milan already leading by two goals to nil. Wearing his now famed No 45 shirt, Balotelli replaced Honduran international David Suazo.

He made a few deft touches but did not really have enough time to make any major impact. But getting a touch of the first team and playing alongside stars such as Maicon, Esteban Cambiasso and Walter Samuel certainly helped his confidence and development. The victory was hardly unexpected – Inter went into the match as Serie A leaders while their hapless hosts were rooted at the bottom.

ESPN summed up the result, saying, 'Internazionale extended their lead at the top of Serie A to seven points after two second-half goals helped them see off plucky Cagliari. The visitors were unable to find a way through in the first half, but took the lead after 57 minutes through Julio Cruz before former Cagliari striker David Suazo finished off his old side 11 minutes from time. The win saw Inter capitalise on Roma's goalless draw with Torino, while Cagliari remained rooted to the bottom of the table following a third consecutive league defeat.'

When asked about Balotelli later, Mancini declared himself 'pleased' and added, 'He is a boy with a lot of promise and I was glad to be able to introduce him gently. You will be hearing a lot more about him – he has a big future.'

That last bit would certainly prove to be correct – by 2012 Balotelli would arguably be one of the five most famous players on the planet!

'Mario himself was pleased to have got on the pitch and made his debut,' I was told by an Internazionale source. 'This is what he had dreamed of all those years ago and what he had worked towards. Many people see him as a loose cannon but I can tell you that he has always been very focused and determined to get what he wants. He is not as maverick as you might believe.'

Just a few days later Mario truly marked his arrival on the scene by scoring twice as Inter won 4-1 at Reggina in the

Italian Cup. Now he had really come of age. He wore the No 44 shirt for the match and shared Man of the Match honours with co-striker Hernan Crespo who would, of course, later in his career play for Chelsea.

Inter's own website, www.inter.it.com, talked excitedly of the impact made by Mario on his first team full debut, 'Inter's road to a fourth consecutive Tim Cup final began with a 4-1 victory over Reggina at the Stadio Granillo. Hernan Crespo opened the scoring early on, with Mario Balotelli adding a second on the half hour. Leonardo Pettinari halved Inter's lead shortly after half time, but Santiago Solari capped a fine performance to restore the two-goal advantage.

'Balotelli completed the rout in the closing stages with his second of the game to make it a full debut to remember. Roberto Mancini fielded a mixture of experience and youth in Reggio Calabria, handing starting debuts to Inter Primavera pair Fatic and Balotelli in a 4-4-2 formation that included Rivas and Pelé, and bringing on Puccio, Maaroufi and Napoli in the second half.'

It certainly was 'a full debut to remember' for Mancini's protégé. Two goals and praise galore – with Mancini patting him on the back as he came off the pitch and later describing his display as 'superb'. Mancini was no late convert to the Balotelli cause – he had been convinced since he first watched him as a 15-year-old in the Inter youth team that the boy would go on to great things and he was also convinced that Mario would deliver the goods for him.

The first instalment of that expected payback had come early – on his full debut. 'Mario was buzzing after the game,' I was told. 'He enjoyed the acclaim after scoring the two goals and now just wanted it all to continue. He wished the match hadn't ended – he wanted to carry on playing!'

But it would be two goals he scored in the next round of the Italian Cup that would really propel him into the national consciousness. Mario was on target against the mighty Juventus as Inter went on to win 3-2 in Turin to book their place in the semi-finals.

The date was 8 January, 2008, and the Italian papers and blogs led almost as one with the headline 'A Star Is Born'. The first leg at the San Siro had ended 2-2 and Mancini decided Mario would be his secret weapon in the return, choosing him ahead of David Suazo.

Many pundits believed Mancini would now approach the tie cautiously but he surprised them by sending out Balotelli in an attacking line-up. *Soccerlens* journalist Marco Pantanella highlighted the belief that Mario was set for greatness with his piece on the 3-2 win. He said that, yes, a star had been born and added, 'His name is Mario. Born in Palermo in August 1990 from Ghanaian parents, he is officially adopted by the Balotellis...His height is 1m 89, his weight 88kg, his touch and technique already reminiscent of the greats of football history. On Wednesday this week, he officially became the Inter Milan hero when the Nerazzurri knocked Juventus out of the Coppa Italia, thanks to two goals by the young striker and a penalty shot by Cruz. Some might say he is Inter's response to a certain young Brazilian recently acquired by AC Milan, but Mario Balotelli is unique in his own way and this week, has proven that your name doesn't have to be Alexandre Pato for everyone to say "A Star is Born in Milan"...

'It must be a real relief for Roberto Mancini, to know

that if (for some obscure impossible science-fiction-like reason) Zlatan Ibrahimovic were to stop scoring all these goals for Inter, there's someone on the bench ready to step in. And shine very very brightly, if only you give him a chance...'

The goals that made the Italian football nation sit up came in the 10th and 53rd minutes. For the first, Mario beat a defender and hammered the ball home, his powerful physique paying off. For the second, he took the ball with his back to the goal, turned and powered it home. It was a terrific strike, earning him the adulation of his team-mates as they mobbed him in admiration.

The official Inter website was also very complimentary about the two goals, saying, 'Inter edged Juventus 3-2 in a pulsating clash at the Stadio Olimpico to complete a 5-4 aggregate victory and set up a Coppa Italia semi-final meeting with Lazio. Inter Primavera's 17-year-old striker Mario Balotelli gave the Nerazzurri a dream start to the third "derby d'Italia" of the season, controlling Maniche's ball into the box and shrugging off a challenge from Birindelli before sidefooting past Belardi for his third goal in the competition...

'Inter were back in front in the 54th minute when "Super-mario" Balotelli collected Stankovic's ball into the area, swivelled and thrashed his shot into the top right corner.'

Mario Balotelli was 17 years old and wasn't just making ripples – no, he was arriving on the scene like a juggernaut. He was big and confident and refused to be jostled off the ball by the equally big but far more cynical defenders that Italy is famed for. He was a boy in a man's body – a tough, physically imposing man. In that sense, he reminded many pundits in Italy at the time of Cristiano Ronaldo, who shares his physical attributes and eye for goal.

Naturally enough, Mario's first goal in Serie A would soon follow. It came in April 2008 in the 2–0 away win at Atalanta. By now he was back wearing his favoured No 45 shirt and he was breathing down the necks of the established strikers at the club. Crespo, in particular, appeared put out that Mancini was pushing the young Balotelli into the team whenever he could.

It was Crespo who would start up front with Balotelli, but the Argentinean made it clear he thought his fellow countryman Julio Cruz should have been his attacking partner. In the second half Mancini would substitute Cruz for Crespo, much to the latter's obvious discontent.

Not that that worried Roberto one bit: he was a man and a manager well aware of how players could act up...after all, he had certainly done enough of that himself in his own playing days! He was oblivious to Crespo's emotions – all that mattered was getting the result and if that meant Mario was the man who would help achieve that better than Cruz, then so be it.

And Roberto would be vindicated as Balotelli once again took the accolades. He set up the first goal for Patrick Vieira and then scored the second himself. But even Mario was not excluded from Mancini's tunnel vision approach to winning. Seven minutes from time Roberto decided Mario was tiring and even subbed him, bringing on Luis Figo in his place!

The win meant Inter remained four points clear of Roma at the top of the league with 72 points – and now looked firm favourites to take the title.

The appropriately-named Italian football journalist Anna

Italia, of Italian Soccer Serie A blog, pointed out the match proved once again that Balotelli was becoming undroppable in the Inter side – and that his star was rising with each game under his belt. Anna said, 'It was an intense match. Yet, it took Inter 20 minutes to break Atalanta's defence. In the 21st minute, 17 years old striker Mario Balotelli makes an assist to midfielder Patrick Vieira who heads from the centre of the box to the very top right corner. It was interesting to see the "silent reaction of Hernan Crespo" when Inter coach Roberto Mancini substituted him in the 57th minute for striker Julio Cruz. Hey, Crespo was not happy because he walked straight past Mancini who just padded his back as saying "well done."

'In the 74th minute, midfielder Dejan Stankovic sends an assist to Mario Balotelli who shoots from the centre of the box to the bottom right corner. What a day for Balotelli. First he provides the assist for the first goal, then, he scored the second goal. What else could he ask for?'

Balotelli was delivering regularly and Inter now went on to win the Serie A title. Mario had won his first major honour at the age of 17. But it was another big-name striker who would make sure that the title returned to the San Siro boardroom. Yes, the mighty Swede, Zlatan Ibrahimovic, returned from a two-month lay-off to claim the win that meant Inter finished just above Roma.

He scored twice in the must-win final game at Parma after only coming on as a sub at half-time. Drawing 0-0 at the interval, Inter were at that stage behind Roma in the battle for the title. But goals from Ibrahimovic in the 62nd and 79th minutes meant that the Nerazzurri clinched their 16th Scudetto – and their third in a row. Once again, Mancini had stood by Balotelli, picking him in his starting line-up even when Ibrahimovic was raring to go on his comeback.

Mario celebrated the title win as energetically as any of his team-mates. He was overjoyed – what a first season in the big time it had been. But just as it seemed he had arrived and would now go on to become an all-time great at Inter, an unexpected dark cloud would appear on the horizon – and it went by the name of Jose Mourinho.

After becoming the club's most successful manager in 30 years, Roberto Mancini was about to be sacked by Internazionale. The man who had become a mentor and a minder for Mario would soon be gone – and he would be left to deal with an altogether darker, more Machiavellian individual. A man who would not take the time or make the efforts to wrap Mario in cotton wool and defend him against any criticism to aid his development. No, Mourinho was very much a man whose ego declared there could only be one idol at any club he worked – himself. From the moment he walked through the door, Mario was living on borrowed time at Internazionale. From being the boy who could be a hero, he had now become an irritant and eventually 'unmanageable' to the new manager.

Mancini had been at the club for four years and had won three consecutive Serie A titles (an Inter club record) and a European record 17 consecutive league game victories stretching nearly half a season. Again he guided Inter to the Coppa Italia final, but lost for a second consecutive season to Roma, 2–1 at the Stadio Olimpico. His time was officially up on May 29, 2008, when Inter put out a statement announcing his sacking.

It was an undignified end to his career at the San Siro and, surely given his record, unwarranted. But while Mancini walked away to lick his wounds confident his reputation as a top-class manager had not been affected – and confident too that he would eventually walk into another top job – Mario eyed the future with some trepidation. He knew of Mourinho and his reputation – and he was also sad that his mentor Mancini had gone. What should have been a summer of holidaying fun turned into one clouded by the shock sacking and the fear of the unknown with the Portuguese man of war.

CHAPTER THREE

MOURINHO MAYHEM

What should have been an easy-going, fun summer for Mario Balotelli proved somewhat less enjoyable as he weighed up the imminent arrival of new Inter Milan boss Mourinho. With mentor and surrogate father figure Mancini gone away into self-enforced retirement (for a season at least), Balotelli wondered what the future would hold for him – as, to be fair, did all the Internazionale players that summer.

Would he fit in with Mourinho's plans – or would he fail to gel with the Portuguese? At least there was one big boost for Mario that early summer of 2008 – when Inter approached him to let him know that they wanted him to sign a new deal, so pleased was club supreme Moratti with his efforts. It was a deal signed before Mourinho arrived – probably just as well, you might say, given the benefit of hindsight about how the two of them so consistently rubbed each other up the wrong way!

It was confirmed by Inter that they had signed him on a three-year contract that would take him through to June 2011. 'Mario Balotelli has signed a new contract with F.C. Internazionale that ties him to the club until 30 June 2011,' the club said. 'The documents were registered at the Italian Football League's offices this morning.'

Agence France-Presse (AFP) commented, 'Balotelli made a massive impression in 2007/08 after being given a first-team opportunity. He played an important part in Inter holding their nerve in the run-in to the title, and his pace and power allowed him to score an impressive seven goals in 15 matches. 12 August will be doubly significant, because when he turns 18 he will qualify for an Italian passport and the right to compete for the national teams. He has already turned down various offers from Ghana and had he celebrated his birthday before August, there was a realistic chance that he may have been included in Pierluigi Casiraghi's squad at the Olympic Games in Beijing.'

Delighted Mario may have been about his new deal – and certainly it left him more settled and at ease at the club – but now he had to convince his tough new Portuguese boss that he was the boy-man to do the business for him. That he was good enough to lead the attack in tandem with the already established No 1 striker, Zlatan Ibrahimovic.

Mourinho arrived at the San Siro for pre-season training in the summer of 2008 and promised that he would give all the existing players at the club a fair chance to prove themselves under him. Whether he truly meant it or not is highly debatable – particularly with the younger players like Mario.

Certainly when he first arrived at Chelsea – and indeed throughout his tenure there – he never really struck me as a man who wanted to nurture and develop young talent. The thing is this with Jose: he is a short-termist. He likes to arrive at a club, win trophies with players who are at their peak – whether they are already in the squad or need to be brought in expensively – and then move on.

He never developed a youth policy at Chelsea that would pay dividends in the years after his exit – nor did he do so at Inter Milan. So Mario was right to be cautious about the new manager's arrival. The *Telegraph*'s talented writer Rory Smith superbly summed up the essence of 'Mourinhoism' when he commented on his tenure at the San Siro, saying, 'It is not to denigrate Mourinho's gifts to accuse him of short-termism. That is what he does, and he does it better than anyone. Take his signings at Inter in the summer of 2009, before his last, silver-laden season: Diego Milito, Wesley Sneijder, Samuel Eto'o. Hardly building for the future. He rarely used Inter's young talents – Davide Santon remains the most obvious – and even his training methods were designed to produce results simply for that one campaign. His successors found a squad short on conditioning, thanks to Mourinho's rigid adherence to a training plan short on stamina work.'

In his first full season at Inter, Mario had made 15 appearances and scored seven goals – a respectable return of a goal every other game. In his first season under Mourinho, he would play in double the number of games of his first campaign, a total of 30, and hit the back of the net nine times. So his appearances were more frequent, but his goals less so – now registering at the rate of one every three games, instead of two.

Mourinho had arrived on a three-year contract and within three months had won his first Italian honour, the Supercoppa Italiana – in no small part thanks to the efforts of Balotelli, who came on as a second-half substitute for Figo. After 80 minutes the match appeared to be heading for a 1-1 draw and extra time. Sulley Muntari had put Inter ahead on 18 minutes, only for Daniele de Rossi to equalise on the hour. But as extra-time loomed, the match unexpectedly sizzled into life. Mario put Inter ahead once again with seven minutes remaining and, right at the death, Murko Vucinic saved the day for Roma. Extra time failed to find a winner and so it was down to the lottery of penalties.

Inter now finally put the tie to bed, winning 6-5 from the spot. Mario again played his part, banging home the second penalty. As the Associated Press (AP) reported at the time, 'Serie A champions Inter Milan defeated Italian Cup holders AS Roma on penalty kicks to win their fourth Italian Super Cup. Roma captain Francesco Totti, in his first game back after a knee injury in April, missed his penalty that would have given his side victory. Roma came from behind twice in regulation time in front of 43,000 spectators at Milan's San Siro stadium. The two teams failed to score in extra-time. Inter regained the cup which was launched in 1998 and pits the winners of Serie A against the winners of the Italian Cup. Mario Balotelli scored in the 83rd with an easy shot when he found himself one-on-one with Roma goalkeeper Alexander Doni after an offside trap failed.'

Mourinho, who had spent most of the match stuck to the bench, was delighted with Mario and the team. His premise on arriving at any club has always been to win some silverware – however small it may appear at the time – just to get something on the board, and in the trophy cabinet. This was his first trophy win through a penalty shootout and probably the high point of his relationship with Mario. He knew the boy had real talent and had seen him apply himself and help win the trophy. He could ask no more of him...yet, at least.

Heading towards December 2008, Mario cemented his relationship with Mourinho by scoring his first Champions League goal. He netted the first goal in the 3-3 draw with Cypriot side Anorthosis Famagusta, at the same time entering the record books as the youngest Inter player (at 18 years and 85 days) to score in the Champions League. His feat eclipsed the previous record set by Obafemi Martins at 18 years and 145 days.

If the goal against the Cypriots was the highlight of Balotelli's second season in the senior squad at Inter, there was no quibbling at all over what were the low points. The first came a couple of weeks after the Christmas decorations had come down – in the middle of January 2009 when he had his first major run-in with Mourinho. The Portuguese was unhappy with Mario's post-Christmas work on the training field and felt that his attitude had deteriorated too. It all came to a head with Mourinho blowing his top and wringing his hands in despair. Fifa.com reported, 'Teenage Inter Milan star Mario Balotelli has paid for his poor attitude with coach Jose Mourinho excluding him from first team action until the end of the month. The 18-year-old son of Ghanaian immigrants is considered to be Italy's finest young talent and has already played for the Italy U-21 side four times, scoring three goals.

'The striker broke into the Inter side during the second half of last season and has seen regular playing time alongside star Sweden forward Zlatan Ibrahimovic during this campaign. However Mourinho, a stickler for discipline, dropped him from his squad, criticising Balotelli's application to training, and on Monday he revealed that things have not improved.'

Mourinho said, 'Nothing has changed, neither Balotelli's way of training nor his attitude. His brother (and agent) has made it clear that Mario wants to go out on loan but I will wait until the end of the transfer window after which he will understand that he has to stay. Maybe then he will change his attitude and return to the first team fold.'

Mourinho was still of the belief that Mario could be one of the best players in the world – but said he needed to apply himself more seriously. 'As far as I'm concerned a young boy like him cannot allow himself to train less than people like [Luis] Figo, [Ivan] Cordoba or [Javier] Zanetti,' said Mourinho. 'I can't accept that from someone who is still a nobody, who hasn't made it yet, who is still a talent with potential. He needs to train harder, to understand what are the important things for me which I think are important for him and his future.

'Because if he was to train half as hard as players like Zanetti and the others, he would be one of the best in the world. But he only trains 25 per cent as hard. Hence in January he will definitely stay here to learn how to train well.'

Mourinho suspended him but kept him at the club, refusing all further pleas for him to go out on loan elsewhere. That in itself was, of course, a major compliment – why would you keep someone unless you thought they were talented? Mourinho had already said he thought Mario could be one of the world's best – and now he was determined to push him hard to achieve that end. That the peace between them would never be established and that they would continue to fall out during a spell that would see Mourinho bring the ultimate club trophy, the Champions League, to the club says a lot about their similar personalities and egos.

Milan simply was not big enough for the both of them – both wanted to be the main man, the star, the darling of the fans but that was never possible with a manager like Mourinho, who insisted on total control and taking total credit for any success.

In April 2009 Balotelli scored Inter's goal in the 1–1 draw with Juventus and was racially abused by Juventus fans throughout the game, with chants such as 'Black Italians do not exist'.

Inter supreme Massimo Moratti was furious at the treatment of his star young player, saying he would have ordered his team to leave the field of play if he had been present. 'If I had been at the stadium, at a certain point I would have left my seat in the stand, I would have gone onto the pitch and I would have pulled the team off,' Moratti told *Gazzetta dello Sport*.

'They seemed proud and happy to sing those things. This is terrible.'

Juve president Giovanni Cobolli Gigli apologised to Balotelli and Inter and admitted Serie A had a problem with racism – and that the culture of racism among fans had to end. 'On behalf of Juventus and the great majority of our fans I want to strongly condemn the racist chanting against Inter Milan's Mario Balotelli,' he said. 'There are no excuses or justification for this type of behaviour. Episodes such as this are inexcusable. Together we must all try to promote a sporting culture that puts respect for the adversary at its core and fights against racism.'

Reuters reported that 'racist abuse is not uncommon in Italian soccer and small fines are usually handed out'. But this time the Italian football authorities finally showed their teeth, as the BBC reported, 'Juventus have been ordered to play a home game behind closed doors after their fans racially abused Inter Milan striker Mario Balotelli at the weekend. The 18-year-old scored Inter's goal in the 1-1 Serie A draw and was taunted by sections of the Juve crowd in Turin. The Italy under-21 international was born in Palermo, Sicily, but is of Ghanaian descent.

'The Italian League is likely to bar fans from Juve's home game against Lecce on 3 May...the abuse suffered by Balotelli on Saturday prompted league officials to come down heavily on Juventus.'

An Italian League statement read: 'The sporting judge considered that in the course of the game and on multiple occasions, fans of the home team, in various sections of the stadium, sang songs which included racial discrimination. Juventus are therefore obliged to play one game behind closed doors.'

The statement, in conjunction with the Italian Soccer Federation, added that the abuse was 'deplorable' and could not be excused as sporting passion.

Balotelli was understandably upset and angered by the incident, but at least he had the satisfaction of knowing his goal had as good as knocked second placed Juve out of the title race. With just six games now remaining, Inter were 10 points clear of their bitter Turin rivals.

The *Telegraph* explained what had led to the racist outburst, saying, 'He [Balotelli] angered home fans throughout the game, particularly for his role in the dismissal of Juve midfielder Tiago. Balotelli was playing keep ball on the touchline with Sulley Muntari, when Tiago let his frustrations get the better of him and kicked both of them, earning a straight red card. Balotelli, who fell down from Tiago's fairly innocuous kick, earned the wrath of a small section of the home fans.'

Of course, Mario's actions in no way excuse the reaction: racism in any shape or form in football is deplorable – as Marcello Nicchi, president of the Italian Referees' Association (Aia), agreed at the time, 'There are 16,000 matches played in Italy every weekend, we have to send out the right signals and educate the people,' he said. 'The racist chants directed at Balotelli are very serious; Uefa and Fifa are always talking about eliminating them. Referees don't have the power to stop a match but they can report on the events to the right authorities.'

Fans in England got their first look at Balotelli in February 2009, when Mourinho lifted the suspension on the player and he came on as a sub in the Champions League first leg against Manchester United at the San Siro. The match ended 0-0 and Mario made little impact, having only 13 minutes to show his worth.

In the return leg at Old Trafford a month later – Mario's first appearance in England – he started the match, lasting 70 minutes until he was replaced by veteran Luis Figo. United won 2-0 and both Balotelli and Mourinho would exit Manchester disappointed and frustrated. Mario had at least set up Ibrahimovic for what was arguably his team's best first-half chance, but the Swede blew the ball wide of Edwin van der Sar's goal. So it was United who went into the last eight of the Champions League – although Mourinho would have more luck the next season, the one in which Inter finally won the competition for the first time in its present format.

Mourinho praised the character of his team, including even Balotelli whom he had previously lambasted for a lack of application, and added, 'United scored two goals over the course of the two games and we have to accept that, in football, the team that wins always deserves it but I don't think we should be negative about my team's display. We played a great match against a great team. We just lacked that little bit of luck you need to win, that little thing that makes that difference between winning and not winning.

'We went one down after a couple of minutes but we had three chances to score in the first half, more than our opponents, and we hit the bar from 10ft out. In the second half we lost another goal but we continued to play and we showed great character.'

Mourinho sounded a little deflated but issued a rallying cry to Mario and his team-mates, telling them they would now at least go on to collect a fourth consecutive Serie A crown back in Italy. They were still top of the table, seven points clear of second-placed Juventus. 'We have not been good enough to win the Champions League but we are good enough to win the Scudetto and I'm sure we will go on and win it,' he said before leaving Manchester with his team.

The Portuguese was right about that – his team did go on to win the Italian league again (the first time under his tenure). Mario had, understandably, been low after the defeat in Manchester but celebrated with his team-mates after they confirmed their Serie A title triumph with a strolling 3-0 win over minnows Siena on 17 May, 2009. AC Milan had lost 2-1 away at Udinese the previous day to set the scene for Inter's 17th Scudetto.

It was a day of personal triumph for Balotelli. He scored one and set one up for co-striker Ibrahimovic. Mario's free kick was deflected after 43 minutes, falling in the path of Zlatan, who could hardly miss.

Balotelli then made it 2-0 on 51 minutes, taking the ball round Gianluca Curci before sliding it calmly inside the near post. Inter would eventually finish 10 points ahead of rivals AC.

The 2009/10 season would turn out to be the last at the club for Balotelli and Mourinho. Both would leave in the summer of 2010, with Jose heading for Real Madrid and Mario, of course, on his way to Manchester City and an emotional reunion with his mentor, Mancini.

Mario's last season at the San Siro saw him make a further 39 appearances for Inter, with him grabbing a total of 11 goals in three competitions (Serie A, the Italian Cup and the Champions League). Predictably, given the natures of Mario and Jose, it was a season packed with incident, controversy and disputes between the two of them.

In November, Inter drew 1–1 against Roma and Mourinho lashed out verbally at Mario for his showing, saying he was 'close to a zero rating'. Mirko Vucinic had put Roma ahead in the 13th minute but Samuel Eto'o – who had arrived at Inter from Barcelona in a swap deal that involved Ibrahimovic going in the opposite direction – earned his new team a point early in the second half. Balotelli had replaced Patrick Vieira at half-time.

The defeat left Inter five points behind second-placed Juventus and Mourinho moaned, 'It has been an awful game from everyone. There was a team that was unable to win, another team that didn't want to win and someone else [the referee] who made too many calls. I didn't like the game. The only thing that I liked was the result. We took a point at home against a team that has quality like Roma and that is fine.'

But his view of Balotelli was far from fine. He rapped, 'Balotelli? In my opinion he came close to a zero rating. I didn't like how he played. He is 19 but could have done much better.'

They were hardly the sort of words that would endear him to Mario. The battle lines had now been drawn and Balotelli would continue to push Mourinho to the limit. The two endured an uneasy peace as the 2009/10 season wore on. At least Mourinho was one of the first to support Mario when he once again fell foul of abuse from the fans of Juventus (who had, of course, racially abused him the previous season).

Inter lost 2-1 to Juve in Turin on December 5, 2009. It was sparked off when Juve midfielder Felipe Melo elbowed Mario in the shoulder – with Mario falling on to the ground as if he had been shot. He held his face in apparent agony and was booked by an unimpressed referee. Melo, meanwhile, was sent off for a second yellow card. Mourinho refused to condemn Mario for his part in the blow-up.

But the duo were back at loggerheads when Inter travelled to Jose's old club, Chelsea, for the second leg of their Champions League knockout clash in March, 2010. Mario did not travel to London after a fresh row with Mourinho, as The *Guardian* explained, 'Inter – with whom he [Mourinho] claimed the domestic title last season – may top Serie A again, albeit by a solitary point, but the 47-year-old is enduring a relatively torrid time in Italy at present. Defeat at lowly Catania last Friday has allowed Milan to gain ground in the championship race, while Mourinho and his Italian striker Mario Balotelli were reportedly embroiled in a spat at training in Milan today which has resulted in the forward being omitted from the squad for disciplinary reasons. Carlo Ancelotti has since suggested he might seek to work with Balotelli at Chelsea.'

The latter never happened – but other Inter Milan players were now quick to criticise Mario. Inter captain Javier Zanetti said after Inter's win at Chelsea, 'We need everyone. If Balotelli saw the game, then he needs to realise how you stay in this team. If that's the way he can feel important in the squad, then he can help us too.'

And Marco Materazzi also got in on the act, telling Sky Sport Italia: 'He should send one [a message] to us instead and thank his team-mates who got him to the quarter-finals. If he wants to be a part of this group, we are happy because he is a really strong player, but if he wants to go somewhere else, the door is open. The president has already shown that he won't hold back anyone who wants to leave.

'It's not true that we don't love him – we love him a little too much. He must be a fan of this team because the president treats him like a son, and so do I. This is our group, if he wants to be a part of it.'

Only Inter supremo Moratti came out with unconditional support of Mario, who was always one of his favourites at the club, but backed Mourinho's decision to axe him from the trip to London. 'Mourinho made the right decision, so it means someone else did not do the right thing for the club,' he said. 'As I consider Balotelli to be a player of immense talent, I trust he will now prove he is a great professional and Mourinho will be very happy to field him again.'

It was becoming clear that Balotelli and Mourinho would not be able to work together – the only question on many pundits' lips in Italy was when the break-up would come. Mario did not help his own cause – in March 2010, he made a terrible blunder when he appeared on an Italian comedy show in an AC Milan shirt. Now he had not only fallen foul of Mourinho, but also his own fans who took none too kindly at him appearing in the shirt of their most bitter rivals.

The website Yahoo Sport summed up Mario's moment of true madness, saying, 'As if Inter Milan teenage striker Mario Balotelli didn't have enough problems as it is, what with all of Italy hating him and his constant spats with Jose Mourinho, wearing the shirt of his club's most hated rival probably wasn't the best way to solve his problems. But that's exactly what he did on Italian comedy show *Striscia la noticia* after they presented him with their jokey Tapiro d'Oro award for not playing in Inter's Champions League win over Chelsea or last weekend's draw against Palermo.

'After giving him the fake golden statue, they then gave Balotelli an AC Milan shirt featuring his name and number, much to the delight of the self-proclaimed Milanista. The *Striscia* cameras later caught Mario wearing the shirt, causing his agent to get defensive, saying he is a "boy of 19 who may not understand the consequences of what he does" and "I hope the fans understand that you cannot take a program like *Striscia* seriously".'

They didn't and Mario was now forced to make a very public apology on the Inter Milan website. It read, 'I am sorry for the situation that has been created recently. I am the first person who has suffered because I adore football and I want to play, and now I am waiting in silence so I can return to being useful to my team. I want to put the past behind me, look to the future and concentrate on the upcoming commitments and make myself ready.'

They were words of contrition...but did Mario mean them? Maybe he did at the time, but his subsequent actions suggested he did not fully appreciate the precariousness of his situation. That any more indiscretions could see him out the door – especially if he got on the wrong side of the people who matter most at any football clubs. Yes, the fans who ultimately pay the players' wages.

The point of no return would come in the Champions League semi-final first leg against Barcelona in Milan on April 20, 2010. Just a fortnight earlier it had seemed Mario was back on track and living up to his pledge to have turned over a new leaf – as he scored in the 3-0 win over Bologna. CNN reported on his triumphant return, saying, 'Young striker Mario Balotelli made a goalscoring return to Inter Milan's line-up as the Italian champions bounced back from last weekend's defeat to maintain a one-point lead in Serie A on Saturday. The 19-year-old was welcomed back into the squad after apologising during the week following his falling-out with manager Jose Mourinho, and helped Inter stay ahead of Roma with a 3-1 victory at home to Bologna.

'It was a successful end to a mixed week for Mourinho, who had announced his unhappiness with Italian football before Wednesday's 1-0 win over CSKA Moscow in the first leg of the Champions League quarterfinals. Brazilian midfielder Thiago Motta put Inter ahead in the 29th minute with the first of his two goals, firing in a shot from the edge of the penalty area after controlling the ball on his chest. Balotelli marked his first outing since March 7 with the second seven minutes after halftime with a cool finish following a pass from strike partner Diego Milito.'

But on 20 April, he fell from grace spectacularly amid the euphoria of Inter's 3-1 win over Barca at the San Siro, a vital result as they would then go on to win the Champions League. Mario had only come on as a late sub and lost his temper after Inter fans groaned when he made a mistake. At the end of the match, he took off his Inter shirt and threw it to the ground in a gesture to the fans.

They did not like it. His career with the club was now as good as over – the necessary bond between players and fans had been broken for good. There would be no way back this time. Mario Balotelli had run out of excuses at Internazionale.

Italian sports newspaper La *Gazetta dello Sport* explained the breach in this way, 'The misunderstanding with the Nerazzurri fans started when Mario misplayed a counter-attack: the lad, on hearing the complaints from the stands, was not impressed. And he lost his head, insulting the fans (reading his lips made that clear) during and after the match. There were also some tense moments an hour after the end of the match. The striker went down to the parking garage to get into his car and leave San Siro, but a group of fans approached him, insulting him and trying to attack him. Security personnel from the club managed to move the aggressors away so that the player could leave the stadium.'

When he most needed support, Mario now found none. Captain Zanetti led the chorus of disapproval, saying, 'Mario needs to focus on doing what he can do on the pitch, he can't allow himself to behave like this. He needs to be intelligent and understand that the fans, at a match like this, can be edgy.'

Inter's managing director Ernesto Paolillo said, 'Balotelli's gesture? Appalling, absolutely appalling. It is something that will need to be discussed.' Then, when the Press pack asked if it would lead to disciplinary action, he barked, 'Absolutely.'

Italian footballing legend Roberto Baggio added to the discussion, saying, 'Balotelli is a great talent, but he needs to change his attitude. Behaving like this does not make him many friends.'

But it was Mourinho who would hammer in the final nail on Mario's coffin as he told RAI, 'I saw an ugly thing. I have been at Inter since July 2009. I remember thousands of pieces of "advice" I got from lots of luminaries in Italy because I wanted to try to educate a talented player. Today in an important showcase like a Champions League semi-final, with the eyes of the world watching, an ugly thing happened.'

It was the end of the road for Mario at Inter: he had burned all his bridges and run out of road. The only thing to be decided now was when he would go and where he would go.

That would soon be answered when Mancini came to his rescue; effectively saving his career and, as history will probably show, saving himself from himself. The only surprise was that he would last longer than his arch enemy Mourinho at the San Siro. Mourinho would become Real

Madrid manager on 31 May, 2010 – just days after taking Inter to that wonderful Champions League triumph at Real's Bernabeu home – while Mario would leave Inter and join Manchester City nine weeks later, on Friday 13 August, 2010.

Friday the 13th...unlucky for some, but not for Mario Balotelli. The boy was about to link up again with his favourite footballing person on the planet – Mancini. Now let's take a closer look at Roberto and his career – and how he crossed paths with Mario, and decided he would take him under his wing and become known as his 'surrogate footballing father'.

CHAPTER FOUR

MANCINI – THE SURROGATE FATHER

We can say with full confidence that no one would play a bigger part in the footballing development of Balotelli than the man who would save him from Italian football by taking him to City – and who would then save him from himself. Step forward Roberto Mancini, Mario's fellow Italian and the man many call his 'surrogate father'.

With good reason…in footballing terms at least. For Mancini would show faith in Balotelli when most managers and pundits within the game in Italy and then England had despaired of him ever sorting out his head. Of him ever controlling the demons that threatened his career. Of him ever showing the talent that God had given him – and that marked him, as Mancini would often claim, as a potential claimant to the title of the best player in the world.

Everyone knew he had the ability, the technique and the

physique to become one of the greatest strikers on the planet. But there were huge question marks over his attitude, his commitment and his character. Only Mancini believed that all the problems could be ironed out; only Mancini believed that, yes, he would fulfil his potential and prove him right. That he would one day be acknowledged as one, if not the, best players in the world – like Messi and Ronaldo.

The most prominent of those who disagreed with Roberto was, of course, Jose Mourinho.

The Special One had voiced his concerns as early as November 2009, claiming Balotelli did not have the mental strength to make it to the top. He felt prompted to criticise the player after Mario had said at a charity event that he actually supported AC Milan, not Inter, and when reports claimed that Mario liked to drive his cars too fast, often above 150mph.

Mourinho said, 'I am the coach of Inter. Someone who does charitable things does it with the heart, not for the publicity and when one of us participates in something I don't understand why the family has to carry the Press behind them. If a player goes and loses two, three or four hours doing a fantastic thing for the people, I don't understand why he has to carry the Press behind him and give an interview. I don't understand because Inter have an organised structure on a Press level. The example is when Materazzi went to visit a prison. I don't understand why a wonderful thing like Balotelli did ends up like this.'

And of his supporting AC Milan, Mourinho added, 'It's not a drama. He was born a Milanista. Inzaghi was born an Interista and he has scored 300 goals for Milan. But the club has a structure and Balotelli represents Inter's future.

Right now, he doesn't have the mental qualities to become a champion.'

And of the driving fast, he said, 'At the beginning of my career I lost an incredible player who was just 20 because he liked to joke around in cars.'

Even when City were about to buy Mario in the summer of 2010, the Portuguese, remarkably, warned them off. Mourinho, by now a year in command at Real Madrid, agreed that Mario had talent but claimed it was outweighed by a bad attitude. Mourinho said, 'The guy has incredible qualities, but sometimes does not know how to use his brain. Let me give an example of when we played at home in the semi-final of the Champions League against Barcelona and he would not take the field. I threw him into the fray and Mario was static, not even giving a hand in defence.'

Replying to what appeared a constant barrage of taunts and criticisms from Mourinho, Mario – perhaps surprisingly – praised Jose but made it clear that he did not rate him in the same league as Roberto when it came to man-management of footballers, class and ability, admitting he much preferred the arm-round-the-shoulder, kid gloves approach of Mancini. 'Mourinho? Among the best,' Balotelli told Italian magazine *L'Uomo Vogue*. 'On a personal level I would say Mancini and then Mourinho. A coach has to bring 100 per cent out of a player and Mancini is brilliant at doing just that.'

In 2012, when speaking to big City fan Noel Gallagher of the band Oasis on BBC Sport's *Football Focus* programme, Mario was asked why Mourinho does not believe in him. Balotelli said, 'That's his problem. They say he wants to come here [to be the manager]. But me, with Mourinho? He's a great manager but he didn't understand me so he said that nobody can understand me. But I think the only one that cannot understand me is him, so it's his problem.'

Of course, some football fans begged to differ with Mario about the relative merits of Mourinho and Mancini – although many others did agree, and said they thought both Mario and Roberto were a breath of fresh air in English football.

One fan, Gary, from Ireland, led the troop of those who backed Mancini, saying, 'Balotelli's just sucking up to Mancini so he doesn't offload him to another club for his past behavior. What has Mancini done to prove that he's better than Mourinho? WHAT??? Typical Balotelli! If he's not acting stupid, he says something stupid!!!'

But City fan Jerry backed Mario, 'As he has played under both managers I am sure he can have his own opinion as too who he prefers. It is obviously Mancini as he likes him and respects him – and Mario we don't believe everything we read. Most of us know you are a true gentleman.'

While another football fan added, 'Balotelli is the best thing to happen to English football since Mourinho.'

Mancini certainly did believe in the boy. He had enjoyed working with him as a youngster at Inter Milan and was determined that he would work with him and see him prosper when he came to England to boss City. He was convinced that the boy had everything that was needed to become a star – and that he just needed someone to believe in him and back him.

Mancini himself is now rated one of the world's top managers and he had certainly put the time in. The 2011/12 season was his tenth as a football manager. A player of great note and talent himself, he started out as a manager in 2001 at Fiorentina, where he stayed for just 12 months before Rome giants Lazio came calling. He worked at the Olympic Stadium for two years before finally moving into the elite of world club football with Internazionale, more commonly known as Inter Milan.

It was in Milan that he would truly forge his reputation as a manager, leading them to three Scudetto (Serie A titles) in a glorious five year spell from 2004 to 2009. He then spent 19 months out of football, recharging his batteries. He was not without offers but was waiting for something really challenging to come along – and it certainly did, when he replaced Mark Hughes as City boss on December 19, 2009.

But there were those in the English media who questioned whether Mancini was the right man for the job – and even whether he was a better bet than Sparky. The *Mail* led the way, saying, 'On the face of it, new Manchester City boss Roberto Mancini boasts an impressive managerial track record in football...But Mancini has enough blots on his managerial CV to surely make even the most ardent critics of the ousted Mark Hughes question the wisdom of the appointment. His reputation has been built on Scudetto wins and, ironically enough, it is there his track record is called into question by some.

'While the history books will record he was Inter's most successful manager in three decades during his time at the San Siro, the first of his titles in 2006 was claimed only after Juventus and AC Milan were stripped of points due to the Italian match-fixing scandal. The relegation of Juve and a points deduction imposed on Milan skewed the subsequent campaign, which Inter won at a canter – 22 points clear of second-placed Roma. While a third title arrived the next year, the writing was already on the wall for Mancini, who had upset the Inter hierarchy with his repeated failure to transfer domestic success into a meaningful Champions League run.'

And Inter president Massimo Moratti made it clear that, in his eyes at least, there would be no reunion for the new City boss and his prodigy Balotelli. Moratti praised City for taking on Mancini but also issued a warning. He said, 'I think City have made a great signing. But they should not inquire about Balotelli for January because we are not selling him.' He pointed out that Mario was under contract until 2011 – but Mario was hardly enjoying his time under Mourinho. In December 2009, he had made just six starts since the previous August, as Jose tried to discipline him and keep him on his toes.

The man who would prove a saviour for Balotelli was born on November 26, 1964, in Jesi, a town in the Marche region of Italy – 20 miles inland from the city of Ancona on the Adriatic coast. His mother, Marianna, a former nurse, and father Aldo, a furniture maker encouraged their son and daughter Stephanie to enjoy their youth and always encouraged Roberto in his love of football. It was a closely-knit community of families and Roberto was always serious about the two activities that would form the bedrock of his life: football and religion. He enjoyed the simple life and traditions of the people who lived in the region – and was known as the 'football boy', because he was invariably seen on the street kicking around a ball.

Growing up he learnt loyalty and the importance of family as a result of living there – and he also learned how important a spiritual background could be in defining a character. He attended mass regularly at the local church and became a devout Roman Catholic – a fact highlighted when just weeks after joining City in 2009, he turned up at St John's Church in Chorlton, south Manchester, for Christmas Eve mass.

Then, in 2012, he took a few days away from City to go on a religious retreat. Under the headline 'It's all to pray for', the *Sun* revealed how the City manager had headed off to Bosnia in March of that year, saying, 'As rival boss Alex Ferguson guided United to victory over Fulham yesterday, City boss Mancini headed to Eastern Europe. The Italian made a pilgrimage with his wife and daughter to Medjugorje in Bosnia and Herzegovina. City could only draw with Stoke at the weekend and have slipped up in recent weeks to hand the advantage to United.

'The Red Devils got a stroke of luck last night when Fulham were denied a definite penalty by referee Michael Oliver at Old Trafford. And Mancini will be hoping for some help from the big man upstairs as the title race hots up.' Football fans throughout the country were intrigued by Roberto's pilgrimage – but one City fan tried to explain why the boss had bothered to go to Bosnia, 'Apparently something happened at this church that made it some sort of hotspot for people into this sort of thing, I'm not a religious guy or a follower so I couldn't tell you what it is as I don't entirely know the details...Mancini is a massive catholic so maybe he feels that this church (for what ever reason) is closer to god and more spiritual? Just think making a story about him praying to god to win the title is a bit too much when the guy has more pressing matters at home regarding family members...

'[And] he most likely went to church because he's a religious man and his father has been ill recently? Maybe he's turned to God because his dad is in a bad way?'

As a youngster, Roberto became an altar boy at the church of San Sebastian and developed his footballing skills on the grass and concrete pitches of the Aurora Calcio boys' club. It was founded nine years before Roberto was born by the church of San Sebastian next door. Roberto honed his skills as an altar boy, and a striker, under the guidance of local priest Father Don Roberto Vigo, now 86. Father Vigo would coach the boys and referee their matches – while Roberto's mother and father would watch him learn from their modest second-floor apartment which overlooked the pitches. Aldo and Marianne would never move from the flat and were always proud of Roberto's achievements in the game.

In January 2010, Aldo told the *Sun*'s Paul Jiggins: 'Like most boys in this area, Roberto's life revolved around football and religion. He was always playing football at the Aurora Calcio. As soon as he came home from school he would be over there, kicking a ball with his friends. There was no stopping him. It was always football, football, football. He used to sleep with his football.

'The only time he didn't have a football with him was when he was carrying out his duties as an altar boy. But then as soon as he was finished at church on Sunday morning, he would change into his football kit and go to the pitch next door to play a match.'

When Roberto was eight he was told that, for one day, he would have to choose religion over football for the occasion of his First Holy Communion – although it didn't end up that way! Aldo said, 'Roberto was a little bit upset because it meant he would have to miss a match. He didn't like it but the First Holy Communion is a big event and all the family came to church to celebrate. It started well but halfway through the ceremony we could not spot Roberto, he was nowhere to be seen. I knew he had sneaked off to the football match and I was very angry. So, at the end of the service, I went over to the priest and apologised for my son leaving. But the priest told me not to worry as he'd asked Roberto to go and play because the team were losing!'

Father Vigo explained, 'I had heard that our team was 2-0 down at half-time. So when I conducted Roberto's communion, I asked him quietly if he had his football kit and boots with him. Roberto said they were in the changing rooms so I told him to sneak out of the side door and put them on because his team needed him. I do not remember the final score but I am sure we didn't lose. I was the first person to coach him and I knew very quickly that he could be something special. He just had something different.'

It was clear that the young Roberto was some footballing talent and it was no surprise when the big clubs' scouts came sniffing around Jesi to see what all the fuss was about with the young boy who was making a name for himself as a prolific striker. Serie A outfit Bologna were the first to make a move for him – signing him at the age of 13. It was a reflection of his commitment and will that he was willing to leave home at such a tender age. He would later say, 'I was very young and it was hard, the first year. My sons are older now, but if I think of them when they were 13, I could not imagine them leaving home. But football was my priority and it changed me.'

Within three years he had progressed so quickly under the watchful eye of youth coach Marino Perani that he was handed his debut for the first team in September 1981, the opening day of the Italian top flight's new season. Mancini was 16 years old – and had the world at his feet, literally. Mancini would go on to make 31 appearances for Bologna that season and grabbed nine goals as his confidence grew.

He was their top scorer and the only ever-present in the team. While Bologna were struggling as a team – they would end up relegated at the end of the season – he was clearly a star in the making, those nine goals earning him the accolade of being the club's top scorer in a season of otherwise despair that had seen them amass a miserly total of just 25 goals.

Other, bigger clubs, in Serie A had spotted that here was a young man with great potential – and he was destined not to drop down a league with relegated Bologna. Instead, Sampdoria came calling in the summer of 1982 – he was now on his way to the Stadio Luigi Ferraris. The big time beckoned and Mancini would prove he was a loyal man by now sticking with the same club for 15 years. That, with hindsight, is a boost for Balotelli and Man City – both would like him to stay at the Etihad and form a new dynasty and, as shown by his loyalty and length of service with Sampdoria, he is clearly capable of staying in one place for a long time if he believes it to be the right decision. Balotelli is keen for Mancini to stay because he knows his own future would be safer if that was the case, and City would also go for that scenario because the Abu Dhabi owners are keen for stability. They have stated that they would prefer to emulate Ferguson and United, with one man masterminding a long-term project, than Abramovich and his constant changes of manager at Chelsea.

Mancini would later explain just why he stayed at Sampdoria for 15 years, saying, 'Yes, I spent my life there. They hadn't had much success. I played there for 15 years because I loved that club, and I wanted to win with them.' You don't need to be a rocket scientist to see the parallels between his arrival at Sampdoria and the similarities at City when he turned up at the then City of Manchester Stadium. Both had been starved of major success and both needed someone to gee them up who instantly fell in love with the club: Mancini as a player at the Italian outfit, and as boss with City.

But Roberto had a volatile side to his character – and this is why he can so easily empathise with Balotelli. While many pundits, players and managers – and even fans! - were puzzled why Mancini continually stood by Mario, particularly in the 2011/12 season, the answer lies within Roberto's own character make-up and his unshakeable belief that Balotelli has enough talent to become a world-class performer.

How could he kick Mario out when his own experiences as a young player told him that some young men need a longer rein, need more forgiveness and an arm around the shoulder before they are ready to rule the world? Why did Ferguson never get rid of Cantona at United? The Frenchman broke every rule – including attacking a fan – and yet the United boss insisted he was going nowhere.

Mancini looked back at his own excesses, disciplinary problems and bust-ups as he was learning the game and realised that Mario had a similar tendency to go astray. But just as he always believed in his own abilities to make it as a top footballer, so he maintained to friends and his closest staff at City that Balotelli would come through. That he would mature and prove him right. That he would eventually repay the trust he had put in him. That patience was the key with Balotelli.

Mancini's own indiscretions as a young player were numerous. On the pitch and off the pitch he had run-ins that bring to mind Balotelli's training ground bust-ups with team-mates including Mica Richards. The *Guardian*'s Daniel Taylor would break the news of the bust-up with Richards, saying, 'The two players clashed towards the end of a practice match when Richards accused Balotelli, who was on the same team, of not running hard enough. Witnesses reported that words were exchanged before the two players squared up. Richards, in particular, seemed aggrieved by what had been said and the defender had to be restrained by James Milner and Yaya Touré as he sought to prolong the argument. City's manager, Roberto Mancini, also got involved to keep them apart.

'The incident has been described as minor behind the scenes, where it has been stressed that it was quickly forgotten once the players had returned to the dressing room. They are understood to have shaken hands and Richards responded to the *Guardian* breaking the story by posting a message on his Twitter site describing them as "all good". Richards added: "These things happen in training & we shook hands after. It shows passion!"'

Mancini laughed off the bust-up with Richards while also giving an inkling of how he too had been in similar shoes to Balotelli as a player. Referring to the 'Why always me' T-shirt

Balotelli revealed after scoring in the 6-1 thrashing of Manchester United, Mancini said, 'I ask him, "why always you?" He said it was because he didn't pass the ball to him. It was a really stupid thing. It was nothing. After 10 minutes it was finished. I was always involved in problems on the training ground, with Trevor Francis and Liam Brady at Sampdoria. It happens. When you play a match eight versus eight and you are passionate, it can happen with every team. Not every week, but often.

'Mario and Micah were boxing but they are like twins. They are very good friends. This has happened with Mario four times now. He is the king for this. But it has happened with other players.'

At the time, Roberto showed his real affection for Mario by also cracking another joke about one of the young Italian's other incidents, the setting off of fireworks in his rented house. Mancini joked, 'However, Mario should pay attention, not just about this, but in every situation. We are near Christmas, at the end of the year it is a very dangerous time for fireworks. It is better he stays in the hotel.'

The Richards bust-up was Mario's fourth with a City team-mate at the club's Carrington training centre. The previous December he clashed with former City defender Jerome Boateng after taking exception to a tackle from the man who would move on to Bayern Munich. He also had words with Vincent Kompany after again being angered by a challenge. And he and full-back Aleksandar Kolarov had also squared up to each other – plus there was the run-in with Manchester United's Rio Ferdinand after Mario's gesture at United fans in the FA Cup semi-final at Wembley.

Mario was also accused of clashing with Yaya Toure – although the brilliant midfield ace would deny the claim. On 2 April, 2012, the *Mail* had claimed, 'Mario Balotelli and Yaya Toure almost came to blows in a dressing-room clash as Manchester City's season threatened to implode. The pair had to be pulled apart at half-time as they trailed Sunderland 2-1 at home before a late rally secured a 3-3 draw. Balotelli and Toure had to be separated by Yaya's brother Kolo as they squared up in front of stunned team-mates at the Etihad Stadium. It is believed Balotelli took exception to the midfielder's criticism about his behaviour during the match.

'It is just the latest in a long line of rows between City stars this season as they head towards finishing the campaign without a trophy – despite massive investment by their Abu Dhabi owners.'

That led to TV pundit Alan Hansen also putting the boot in on Mario. In his *Daily Telegraph* column, the former Liverpool defender said, 'If Manchester City really are prepared to sell Mario Balotelli this summer, then it would absolutely be the right thing to do. He has become a damaging distraction at the Etihad Stadium and Roberto Mancini must shoulder the blame for allowing the situation to develop to the point where the player is beginning to affect the unity of the dressing room.

'When you are going for a title, Balotelli and everything that he brings with him goes against everything that you want down the final straight. If he performed like Lionel Messi, Cristiano Ronaldo or even Wayne Rooney, then the players would hold up their hands and let him get away with it. But Balotelli is not a world-beater, he is certainly not playing well at the moment and he is a huge distraction.'

They were harsh words from Hansen – especially as Yaya then faced the public and dismissed the allegations of a bust-up as nonsense. Yaya said he saw Balotelli as a 'brother' and 'loves' him. 'They said I fought with Mario at Swansea and against Sunderland. That shocked me. My lawyers called me about this and it was the first I knew about it. It's just not true. It didn't happen. I am a footballer, not a boxer. People don't know my relationship with Mario. He's not my friend, he's my brother and I love him. To say we had a fight is very sad. It upset me and I feel sorry for Mario. He suffers most from these things.

'At half-time against Sunderland it was very difficult. We are trying to win the league and are losing 2-1. It's not good. But everybody was quiet. We were just looking at each other, trying to find a way to turn the result. But I didn't even talk to Mario. The next day he sent me a text message saying, "Apparently we had a fight". I just want to stop people writing and thinking that.'

And Mancini then also leapt to the defence of his young countryman, saying, 'There are some people who think bad things against other people, like Mario. Every time Mario does something, [it] is like a war. There are other people on and off the pitch that do worse than Mario and no one says anything because maybe they play for an important team or are not like Mario.'

But he did add that Balotelli could solve the problem of being in the papers for the wrong reasons himself – by not getting involved in unsavoury incidents. 'I would like Mario to play, score and finish the other situation,' he added. 'It is not maybe your [the media's] fault – it is his fault because if he wants he can play and stay at home. Like this, no people can ask about the other situation.'

Roberto would clash with three major stars while at Sampdoria – the first coming when he was just 18, with Britain's first million pound footballer, the generally easy-going Trevor Francis. Francis arrived from England as a 28-year-old and Mancini feared the arrival would cost him his place in the Sampdoria starting line-up. Francis takes up the story, 'It happened about a year after I had been there. There was a little incident in a friendly training match that at the time I thought was something and nothing. We had a disagreement on the pitch about it but it continued into the dressing room. We had to be split from each other. Let's just say all the players made sure that it didn't go any further.

'We made up afterwards and there was no ill feeling, after all we played together for another three years.'

Roberto also famously had a slanging match with Liam Brady – who was eight years his senior at Sampdoria – and former Manchester United and Chelsea midfielder Juan Sebastian Veron. The Argentine, then playing as a midfielder at Sampdoria, told how Mancini had verbally abused him over a corner the Italian felt he could have better delivered. When the match finished, Mancini stripped off to the waist and was waiting to fight Veron. Veron would elaborate, 'Once, when I was playing at Sampdoria, I had a terrible argument with Roberto. He is not an easy person, you know. He has this complicated personality. Today, he is a friend of mine and he really helped me during my career. We played together at Sampdoria, Lazio and he was my coach at Inter. But let me tell you our beginning was hard. We were playing for Sampdoria and we were facing Piacenza. I hit a terrible corner kick and he asked me nicely, "Next time, try to kick the ball higher." I don't know why, but I got really furious and then I insulted him.

'So when I entered the dressing room, he was waiting for me. He wanted to punch me! In fact, he had taken his shirt off, and he was ready to fight me as if we were kick boxers! Fortunately, there were some team-mates who didn't let him punch me. I knew that I had showed a bad attitude towards him on the field. So, when he had calmed, I apologised to him.'

A 'complicated personality'...does that remind you of anyone? Maybe his surrogate son Balotelli? It becomes increasingly clear just how and why Mancini is probably the only person on the same wavelength as his fellow Italian – and why he trusts him to come good. He had experienced ups and downs just like Mario. No way was he a little angel.

And then there was Roberto's bust-up with Carlos Tevez. Kia Joorabchian, Tevez's agent, revealed the Argentine striker and his manager almost came to blows following the 2-1 home win over Newcastle in the 2010/11 season. Joorabchian said on behalf of Tevez, 'After last season's home game with Newcastle I had a row with Mancini. We almost hit each other in the dressing room, but the following day we spoke. Mancini is a winner and I am a winner too. None of us like to lose.'

Mancini was also something of a wild lad away from the pitch – at least until he settled down with his wife Federica in 1990. In October 2011, he criticised players in England who like too much drink – but also offered an insight into how he relaxed before meeting Federica! 'I do not understand players drinking until they are drunk. We do not have that culture in Italy. We would prefer to go off with a woman. That's what I liked to do after a match, and I tell my players now it is better that they go with a woman than drink.'

There was another similarity with City's set-up when Mancini arrived at Sampdoria as a player. The club was owned by Paolo Mantovani, a wealthy benefactor who had made his fortune in the oil industry. The ambitious Mantovani had dreams of challenging Italy's football elite – immense wealth and dreams of challenging the footballing elite. Indeed, Sampdoria '82 could have been City '09 when Mancini was drafted in as manager.

Mantovani had bought the club in 1979. Back then they were languishing in Serie B, but his money and enthusiasm turned things around and, by the time Mancini arrived in '82, they were back in the Serie A top-flight.

Now Mancini's fortunes seemed to run parallel to Sampdoria's success. In his first campaign he managed only five goals, then ten in his second and by the third both he and the club were buzzing as they won their first Coppa Italia. Roberto scored from the penalty spot in a 3-1 win over AC Milan to lift the trophy. The quality of the team could be gauged from the fact that the other men on target that day were Graeme Souness and Gianluca Vialli. The money had been spent on team investment – and it had been spent well. The following season Sampdoria again made the Coppa final and Mancini scored again, but this time it would end in disappointment as they lost 3-2 to Roma.

In 1986 Vujadin Boskov was appointed as new head coach and Mancini and the club won their second Coppa Italia in

1988 and a third a year later – the latter being a 4-1 romp over Napoli with both Mancini and Vialli again on target.

In 1990 the two strikers played another key role as they helped Sampdoria to their first European trophy – as they overwhelmed Anderlecht of Belgium 2-0 in Gothenburg, Sweden. Vialli grabbed both goals in extra time to take the trophy to Italy.

But both Mancini and Vialli – and indeed Sampdoria as a club – craved one missing trophy: the Serie A title. They wouldn't have to wait long to get their hands on it. The year after they lifted the Cup Winners' Cup, they won the league, finishing five points ahead of second-placed Inter Milan. The winning team featured several other world-class stars – including Gianluca Pagliuca, Toninho Cerezo, Pietro Vierchowod and Attilio Lombardo.

That left just the European Cup for Mancini and Vialli to win. The following season, they managed to reach the final, but were defeated by Barcelona at Wembley. The website www.dtfoot.com has done an excellent job in setting up the pre-match drama, after pointing out that the final would be the last under the name of the European Cup. The following season would see it rebranded as the Champions League. The Four-Dimensional site said, 'Suitably, the last European Cup final was hosted in Wembley – Europe's most prestigious stadium – and featured two sides who had never won the European Cup before. Sampdoria and Barcelona. For a club with a modest history like Sampdoria, the lack of a European Cup in their trophy cabinet was hardly remarkable. Indeed, the 1991/92 campaign was their first ever participation in the European Cup. Although not traditionally a great club, from the late

80s onward Sampdoria had been busy constructing a side of excellent quality. With players like Gianluca Vialli, Roberto Mancini and Toninho Cerezo, Samp achieved success in Europe (reaching two Cup Winners' Cup finals) and Italy (winning Serie A in 1991). This was the greatest moment in their existence.

'Barcelona present us with a different story altogether. A giant club, with a massive stadium, massive fan supports, and a massive reputation of chronic underachievers. Always lingering in the shadow of Real Madrid, the Catalans had failed to win the European Cup before, despite reaching two finals. But there was a different wind blowing through the Camp Nou. Coach Johan Cruyff had instilled a sense of self-confidence in his players, based on a philosophy of attacking football, which allowed Laudrup and Stoichkov to display all their genius. Could they finally win their first European Cup?'

Unfortunately – for Mancini and co at least – they could. Barcelona won the game 1-0, thanks to a Ronald Koeman free-kick. Mancini had the honour of captaining the side at Wembley but was gutted by the defeat. He had wanted a European Cup medal to complete his trophy room at home, but it was not to be.

At the end of a hard-fought match he trudged off the Wembley pitch – but would not forget the excitement he had felt that night at Wembley, nor the play of his counterpart No 10, one Pep Guardiola. The latter would, of course, go on to become the most successful manager in Barcelona's history and Mancini would follow his progress over the years. He would also remember Wembley and London. 'Even though he was on the losing side that night, he felt something with England and the country's love of football,' I am told. 'He made a vow to himself that one day he would return – whether as a player or a manager. Even then he had plans to become a coach. He is a man who had always known what he has wanted and has been prepared to work hard to get it.'

Sampdoria's league triumph 20 years ago, the only one in their history, was a remarkable achievement in a formidable division, which included European champions AC Milan, big-spending Juventus, a Diego Maradona-led Napoli and an Inter side containing world champions West Germany's three best players – Andreas Brehme, Lothar Matthaus and Jurgen Klinsmann.

The *Manchester Evening News* did a piece on Vialli before the 2011 FA Cup final – and summed up his worth to Sampdoria during his playing days there while also noting his tendency to flare up, 'Mancini's strike partnership with Gianluca Vialli was crucial to Sampdoria success. Indeed, Mancini had become a key part of the club's fabric. When Sven-Goran Eriksson flew to Monte Carlo to be interviewed for the manager's job in 1992, Mancini was part of the interview panel. He was the club captain, he often gave the team talks and he even helped to design the kit. And yet despite all of this responsibility, he still had a capacity for flashes of temper. Eriksson remembers Mancini the player as being "awful" when it came to haranguing referees. One match against Inter Milan in 1995 stands out. Having been denied an early penalty, Mancini went crazy at the referee, then flung off his captain's armband and stormed from the pitch, telling Eriksson he was never going to play again. Having been persuaded by his manager to return, the striker was soon sent off anyway, for a reckless lunge at Paul Ince. He collected a six-match ban.'

Yes, even in 1992, at the age of 28, Roberto Mancini was taking the first steps towards become a manager. He was Sampdoria's captain on the field and was taking increasing responsibilities off it, as his role in the appointment of Eriksson indicated. This was a man born to be a leader. Even former England midfielder David Platt – now of course one of Mancini's first team coaches at City – would learn early on in his career how much of an influence Mancini held at Sampdoria.

In 1991 Platt had joined Italian outfit Bari for £5.5million but only stayed one season as the club were relegated from Serie A. Platt received a phone call from Roberto Mancini in January 1992, asking him to join him at Sampdoria. 'We'd played Sampdoria a few times and I'd faced Robbie,' Platt says. 'But I didn't know him and he'd tracked my number from somewhere. He said: 'I know you've got a good relationship with your president, I'm sure you could push through a move to us.'

Platt, his own man, decided instead to join Juventus, which he did for £6.5million in July 1992. Still Mancini would not give up and a year later Platt finally moved to Sampdoria.

Platt revealed, 'Every two weeks [at Sampdoria] he would be on the phone, pressing me.'

Mancini's persistence would eventually pay off as Platt struggled in and out of a star-studded Juve team. Eventually he was not just ready to listen to Roberto's overtures – he was hoping he would make them, '[Then] Juventus played Sampdoria, Robbie was playing, so I was marking him and hovering around him, hoping he would say something. I've always suspected I wasn't on Sampdoria's list that summer, because their president wanted to sign Marco Osio from Parma but he ran the transfer list past Robbie, who had much of the say. I soon made the move.'

Just as Mancini would help shape Platt's career, so Eriksson would now shape that of Mancini himself. Mancini would learn from the Swede about the technical side of management as he joined Lazio as a player, working under Eriksson. Success continued for Roberto – he won the Serie A title again, the European Cup Winners' Cup and two more Coppa Italias.

But by the new millennium, he had had enough of the playing side and stepped straight into the management side, becoming Eriksson's No 2 at Lazio. In 2011, Eriksson spoke of how Roberto took the role – and how he had a real control freak side to him. Eriksson said, 'I took him to Lazio with me and he wanted to be a manager even while he was a player. He was the coach, he was the kit man, he was the bus driver, everything. At Sampdoria he wanted to check that everything was in place before training. Sometimes I would have to tell him, "Mancio, you have a game to play on Sunday, you will be exhausted if you have to control everything." But he was like that.'

In January 2001 Mancini was tempted out of playing retirement by the prospect of making his mark in England. He was signed by then Foxes boss Peter Taylor, on the recommendation of Eriksson. The Swede by now had taken the job of England boss and Mancini followed him to Blighty. The *Telegraph*'s Henry Winter explained how Mancini's arrival could prove a timely boost for Leicester, the England national team and Mancini himself, 'Mancini's deal is one that suits all parties. Leicester gain a forward capable of holding up the ball and educating Taylor's callow, shot-shy strikers. Mancini, 36, stays fit, learns a bit while waiting to take up a Serie A coaching position in the summer and makes the occasional call to the England coach. Eriksson, who shares an adviser with Mancini and recommended him to Taylor, has another pair of eyes focusing on English football. Everybody is happy.'

Peter Taylor was certainly happy. He told the Press that Mancini's arrival had lifted spirits at Leicester, 'Everyone thinks the world of Robbie because he is such a star in Italy,' said Taylor. 'Muzzy Izzet said he would move out of his mansion, let Robbie move in there and he would go and live in a caravan. Everyone now wants an "o" at the end of their name; Savagio, Izzetio and all that.'

Mancini explained that he had been offered coaching work at Lazio when Eriksson left for England, but that he had refused: 'I was asked whether I wanted to stay and work with Dino Zoff [Eriksson's successor at Lazio] but I said it was more correct to also leave like Eriksson. I had offers from Italy to keep playing which I refused.'

It was then – while at Leicester – that Mancini would truly be 'bitten by the bug' of English football. He was only with the Foxes for a short period of time but he became enchanted by the nature of the game in our country – the passion of the fans, the general honesty of the players and the exciting quality of the play. This was the point when Mancini decided he would one day return as a manager to England. He knew he had what it took to be a success in the managerial game; now he was about to prove it. The man who would also bring Mario Balotelli to

England – because he felt he too was suited to the game over here – was about to launch into the career move that would end with him, and Mario, coming from their native Italy to Manchester City.

CHAPTER FIVE

KISSED BY GOOD FORTUNE

Mancini's time at Leicester would be short and sweet. He joined the Foxes in January 2001 after coming out of retirement, but would only make five appearances before leaving a month later and finally hanging up his boots. He had not made that much of an impact in England and Leicester boss Peter Taylor would feel disappointed that he had left so quickly – but, as we previously touched upon, England had made a big impact on Mancini. 'It was at that point that he decided he would one day like to return as a manager,' I am told by a source. 'Roberto has always had great self-confidence and self-belief – he knew he was talented enough to make it as a head coach, after all, he had been helping Sven out at Lazio and had been one of the decision makers at Sampdoria, even when he was still a player!

'He had seen how Sven had settled into the England job and wanted a taste of it himself – he decided there and then he would return one day and he even admitted he wouldn't mind the chance of one day managing the English national team, given the chance!'

Certainly, Mancini at the time appeared to back up that idea, saying he was keen to improve his mastery of the English language and pick up hints from Taylor and Eriksson (again) on management. He would say, 'It is too early for me to judge Peter Taylor as a manager but he seems very good. He is very honest. I have finished my Italian coaching course, which is recognised by UEFA, so I can now coach an Italian side.' But he did not rule out managing in England, 'When I was a player I was always interested in management. If there is an opportunity to be a coach in England, it's possible I will stay here. English football is very different from Italian; it's more physical and matches are always very open. People talk about the speed of the English game, but in Italy referees blow their whistles very often so you cannot build up speed. In England, referees wave play on and so it becomes faster.'

Taylor himself dismissed the idea that Mancini had just come to the Foxes for the easy money and an easy ride for a few months, 'Robbie's got enough money," he said. 'He hasn't come here for the money. He has come here to do well. If he had been unemployed for five years and living in a one-bed flat in Rome, I would be nervous thinking he was just coming here for the money. But he probably has 500 one-bedroom flats in Rome.'

By February 2001, Roberto had gone from England – it would be another eight years before he returned again, as City manager.

One of his best games for the club would come in the 2-1 win over Chelsea in the Premier League on February 3, 2001. He would play a key role in the win and City's official website would drool over his skills, saying, 'The second period was dominated by the home side and Mancini produced some of the sublime skills that have made him a legend in his homeland. Chances came thick and fast and one breathtaking chipped cross from Mancini appeared to have created Izzet's second goal but the midfielder headed just wide.'

The *Telegraph* summed up his short stay at Leicester, hinting that the time for Mancini to step into the manager's chair was already imminent, 'Robert Mancini has left Leicester City amid reports in Italy that he is poised to become the next coach of Fiorentina. The former Italian international striker, who resigned as player-coach at Lazio when Sven-Goran Eriksson left Rome to become England's new manager, has informed Peter Taylor that he will not be extending his month-long contract with the Filbert Street club. He has cited personal reasons for his decision.

'Taylor had allowed Mancini to return to Italy earlier this week with the understanding that he would be back in time for Saturday's FA Cup fifth-round tie with Bristol City, but he received a phone call from the 37-year-old last night informing him he would not be returning.'

Taylor admitted he felt low about Roberto's early exit. He had enjoyed working with a man who was a super professional and had hoped he would stay around longer and continue to exert his influence on the squad. Taylor would say, 'It's obviously a big blow because we were expecting him to be playing on Saturday. It's an important match. But sometimes these things happen when you bring someone in from abroad. I can't praise Roberto enough for what he did while he was with us.'

Mancini himself would later admit how he enjoyed his brief spell with the Foxes, and confirmed it gave him the taste for wanting to work in England again one day. He said, 'I stayed at Leicester for one month and I really enjoyed my time with the club. If my memory serves me correct, I left with the team in a good position – sixth I think – and I played five games only one of which we lost, to Everton. It was a very good experience for me – short, but enjoyable and it made me want to return to work in England one day.

The Leicester fans were wonderful to me and the players were very respectful and friendly, too.'

The rumour mill was rife that the Italian was heading home for his first role in management – and with a big-time outfit. The coach at Fiorentina, Fatih Terim, had confirmed he was about to leave the job and Mancini was the obvious choice to replace him, having only just lost out to the Turk for the role the previous summer. The Leicester website, www.leicestercity-mad.co.uk, highlighted the likelihood of the move at the time, saying, 'Leicester's Roberto Mancini looks set to quit the club after it was revealed he has been lined up as a successor to Fatih Terim at Fiorentina. The former Sampdoria and Juventus forward is set to have talks with Foxes boss Peter Taylor before returning from Italy. Mancini signed a five-month loan deal at Filbert Street in January and has failed to score so far. The ex-Italy international has made no secret of the fact that he is desperate to move into management and was disappointed not to be considered for the vacant Lazio post. Mancini has been travelling back to Italy every week as he completes his coaching course which is mandatory for Serie A managers and has only been training with Leicester three days a week.

'Terim, current coach at Fiorentina, has announced that he will leave Florence at the end of the season and Mancini is hotly tipped to be his successor after applying for the job last season. Mancini was beaten to the post by Terim when Giovanni Trapattoni left in the summer and it is understood that it was a close decision for the Fiorentina board between the two. Fiorentina vice-president and former editor of the *Corriere dello Sport* newspaper, Mario Sconcerti, dropped the biggest hint, saying: "Mancini was a big player and he will be a big manager".'

The Italian media had another phrase reserved for Mancini – he was *'baciato dalla grazia'* ('kissed by good fortune') as the *Guardian* would reveal: '[It is] how Italians refer to those rare, fortunate individuals who always appear to effortlessly achieve what they want in life. It is a label that has followed Roberto Mancini throughout his career in Serie A. Mancini's flamboyant style as a player, as much as his 202 goals at club level, won him star status among adoring fans in a career that started at Bologna in 1981, included 15 seasons at Sampdoria until 1997 – alongside, among others, Gianluca Vialli – and ended in 2000 after three years at Lazio. His cavalier playing style, full of inventive flicks and daring goals, plus the blond-streaked hair, the tan and the stubble gave him more the air of an Australian surfer than a serious Serie A goalscorer. The glamorous image – he always appeared near the top of polls for "Italy's best looking footballer" and his website declares he is a "Campione di Classe", or Champion of Class – suggest a flamboyant character but those who know him describe him as "a very closed person", while his critics have called him arrogant and vain.'

BBC Sport confirmed at the time that Mancini was indeed likely to get the job in Florence, 'Leicester City have given Roberto Mancini permission to miss their FA Cup fifth-round tie with Bristol City amid speculation he is being lined up to take over as coach of Fiorentina. Mancini says he is back in his native country "to sort out family problems". But reports and sources in Italy suggest that Mancini is being lined up to replace Fiorentina's Turkish coach Fatih Terim. Terim joined Fiorentina after steering Galatasaray to last season's Uefa Cup final triumph over Arsenal. But there are reports he will not be renewing his one-year contract.

'It means Mancini could have already played his last game for Leicester. He is due to hold talks next week with Foxes manager Peter Taylor.'

A Leicester spokesman had confirmed: 'Roberto has kept us fully informed of his situation and is staying in Italy for some extra time. We plan to talk to him early next week.'

While Mancini said: 'I am in Italy to try and sort out family problems. I hope I can and I look forward to playing for Leicester again.'

He would not play for Leicester again. Instead, as predicted and expected, Mancini would now take on his first managerial post at Fiorentina. The club were in financial straits when Roberto took command, yet he would guide them to win the Coppa Italia.

It would be a hands-on, learn-as-you-go experience. Roberto had even needed to get special dispensation from the Italian FA to take the job in the first place – as he was not sufficiently qualified in terms of his coaching badges.

He grafted all hours to turn the club around, to try to save it from financial meltdown by bringing success on the pitch, even donning a shirt and playing for the first team as he also tried to guide the club from the manager's office. 'It was a very stressful time,' a source tells me. 'But Roberto is a tough man; someone who refuses to ever give in and gradually his efforts paid off, he started to turn the club around – and, remarkably, led them to success in the Coppa Italia that would not have seemed possible when he arrived.'

The financial crisis had led to him working unpaid for weeks on end and the fans were not happy when heroes such as Rui Costa and Francesco Toldo had to be sold to balance the books. Mancini lasted just 10 months in the job, quitting in January 2002 with the club second bottom in Serie A. Some pundits have argued that he quit when the going was bad – rather than seeing out the job. But he had brought unexpected success in the Coppa Italia and he was a young man learning his new trade; he wasn't the messiah. Not at that stage anyway...that would only come with Balotelli at City!

Plus there was the little matter of exactly why he said he had resigned. Because he feared for his family's safety after the fans had become angry over the enforced sale of stars to bring in much-needed cash. Mancini said that when he had returned to Florence one night after talks in Rome with Fiorentina owner Vittorio Cecchi Gori he had been 'verbally attacked outside my house by five fans who threatened to intensify the aggression'. He added, 'The fear of creating problems for my wife and my three children has led me to believe that my work in Florence cannot continue. But I hope I have provided a positive contribution, always giving my best. I want to underline the great professionalism and attachment to the club of my players and all my colleagues despite the daily difficulties having reached the limits of normal endurance.'

Roberto's tough mental strength was being moulded yet again. Here was a man who was making his way to the top in the most difficult of situations and drawing strength from his experiences. They would all contribute to making him the manager he would eventually become at Inter Milan – and, finally, City.

Four months after the exacting test in Florence, Roberto would be back in the hot seat – at his old playing club, Lazio. But it would again be a test of character – as Lazio were also suffering financial woes. The European Football governing body, Uefa, informed the international Press that Mancini was back in business in Rome after his fall-out in Florence, confirming, 'Roberto Mancini, the former Italian international, has accepted an offer from S.S. Lazio to take over from Alberto Zaccheroni as head coach of the Roman club for next season, according to reports in Italy. Even though a formal contract will only be signed next week, once Serie A has been concluded, Mancini is believed to have agreed a two-year contract with a salary of €1m per season. Lazio's president Sergio Cragnotti is looking to start a new era after a disappointing season for the club who were eliminated from the UEFA Champions League in the first group stage and who could fail to qualify for both next season's Champions League and UEFA Cup depending on results this weekend, the league's final matchday.

'Mancini made his Serie A debut on 13 September 1981 for Bologna FC against Cagliari Calcio. The 38-year-old went on to play for Sampdoria UC, Lazio and Leicester City FC. He won two Italian first division titles (one with Bologna, one with Lazio) six Coppa Italias (four with Bologna, two with Lazio) and two European Cup Winners' Cups (one with Sampdoria, one with Lazio). For the Italian national team, Mancini won 36 Italian caps and scored four goals. At the end of his playing career, Mancini became Eriksson's assistant coach at Lazio in July 2000. In spring 2001, he took over as head coach of AC Fiorentina after Fatih Terim's departure. However, after a poor start to the season, Mancini resigned from the Florence club in January.'

At Lazio he would feel déjà vu as once again – as at Fiorentina – he was forced to sell off his star men, including Hernán Crespo and Alessandro Nesta, to bring in money at the cash-starved club. But again, he brought success. In his first season, Lazio made it to the semi-finals of the UEFA Cup. They would exit at this stage – and Mancini would for the first time come across a man who would become a major adversary over the years. Yes, the then Porto manager, Jose Mourinho.

Porto would win 4-1 on aggregate – the score after the first leg in Portugal while the second leg in Rome would end 0-0. The Associated Press said after the first leg that there was now the possibility of Portuguese domination in the competition, 'An all-Portuguese UEFA Cup final looked a good bet after FC Porto trounced Lazio 4-1 in their first-leg semi-final on Thursday. Earlier, Boavista held on for a 1-1 draw with Celtic in Scotland. The return legs are in two weeks. "This is great for Portuguese soccer. I'm really happy," said Portuguese Prime Minister Jose Durao Barroso. No Portuguese team has won the UEFA Cup. Neither

Boavista nor Porto had previously passed the quarterfinals, but Porto took a giant step towards the final with an electrifying home victory over the Cup favourites and 1999 champions from Italy.'

Lazio may have been favourites – they were fourth in Serie A and going great guns – but they had no answer to Mourinho that dire night in Portugal. Claudio Lopez had put Mancini's men ahead – only for Derlei to grab a brace and Nuno Manique and Helder Postiga to complete the rout.

'We were better than our opponent today, and that's reflected in the scoreline,' Mourinho boasted while Mancini could only admit, 'It was a tough defeat but we have to keep our hopes up for the second leg. Porto was better all round. We lacked guts at times.'

You wouldn't expect any Mancini team to have 'lacked guts' and certainly he had his men revved up for the second leg. But once again they were unable to get the better of Mourinho. The frustrations of the night were summed up by a missed penalty and a sending off for Roberto's team. Claudio Lopez's penalty was saved by Vitor Baia and defender Cesar was sent off along with Porto's Helder Postiga. Both players had been booked and were then sent off in the first half for separate second booking offences.

Mancini's European dream was over for another year – and, in the event, Mourinho's team would not meet Boavista in the final – they would beat Celtic 3-2 in Seville to lift the trophy, the year before Jose then won the Champions League with the same team.

That first season would also see Mancini lead Lazio to fourth spot in Serie A, a commendable achievement.

The following season Lazio under Mancini would finish sixth in Serie A but would win the Coppa Italia. The final was played over two legs with Mancini's men taking on the legendary Juventus. The first leg was played in Rome on March 17, 2004, with Lazio winning 2–0. The second leg was played on May 12 in Turin and the two clubs drew 2-2, giving Lazio their 4th Coppa win 4–2 on aggregate.

Mancini had come a long way as a manager in a short time – he had led Lazio to the Coppa triumph by outwitting one of the greatest ever Italian managers, Marcello Lippi.

His success with a lack of money had been noted by the elite in Italian football and as the 2004/05 season loomed the rumour mill was rife that Roberto had been asked to take on one of the biggest jobs in Italian football – manager of Inter Milan.

At the San Siro, Roberto would become the club's most successful manager in 30 years, winning three consecutive Serie A titles and the Coppa Italia. Goal magazine would later best sum up his contribution, 'Mancini remains to this day Inter's longest-serving boss under Massimo Moratti. After a third-place finish and a Coppa Italia win in his first season in charge, the president finally got his hands on a Scudetto as a result of the first Calciopoli trial of the following summer. The Nerazzurri would go on to dominate in Italy under Mancini, but he would never see this materialise into success in Europe, and after he told his players he wanted to leave following a Champions League defeat to Liverpool in 2008, his exit that summer was inevitable.'

Mancini led Internazionale to their first domestic trophy since 1989 when he took them to that Coppa Italia success in his first season in 2005. They beat Roma 3-0 on aggregate to secure the crown, winning the first leg 2-0 in Rome and following that up with a 1-0 win at the San Siro. Mancini would lead them to another Coppa win and then three consecutive Serie A wins, in 2006, 2007 and 2008. The win in 06 was the club's first title success in 20 years and Roberto became only the third coach to take Inter to back-to-back league titles after Alfredo Foni (1952–53 and 1953–54) and Helenio Herrera (1964–65 and 1965–66). Of course, there was talk that the '06 win was not that much of an achievement as it was gained by default – Juventus had topped the league in both 04-05 and 05-06 but were stripped of both titles due to an Italian Football Federation ruling regarding match-fixing on July 26, 2006. Inter Milan were awarded the 2005-06 title. No replacement winner was named for 2004-05.

Some pundits thus suggested Mancini's achievement was devalued as it was achieved by default, but that is surely nonsense if results were fixed at the top of the championship!

The scandal was uncovered in May 2006 by Italian police. Juventus were the champions of Serie A and were implicated in the scandal as teams were accused of rigging games by selecting favourable referees. Inter had finished third behind winners Juve and runners-up AC Milan, who were also accused of being involved in the scandal. The BBC summed up the punishments, 'Serie A sides Juventus, Lazio and Fiorentina have been demoted to the second division for their involvement in Italy's match-fixing scandal. Juventus were also stripped of their last two Serie A titles and had 30 points deducted, meaning they are likely to stay down for two seasons. AC Milan will stay in Serie A but will start the season docked 15 points. All are barred from playing in Europe – Juventus, Milan and Fiorentina in the Champions League; Lazio the Uefa Cup.'

CNN reported how Mancini became an unexpected winner in '06, 'Inter Milan have been officially awarded the 2005-06 Italian league title in the latest fallout from the country's match-fixing scandal. The Italian Football Federation's (FIGC) decision to award Inter their 14th title comes after a sports tribunal revoked Juventus' title win from last season.

'Juventus also had their title win from 2004/05 revoked but no replacement winner will be named for that season. The decision to give Inter their first title since 1989 came after a sports tribunal handed down guilty verdicts to Juventus, who had finished top of Serie A, AC Milan who were second and Lazio and Fiorentina.' Inter had finished 15 points behind Juve, who won the title with a record 91 points.

But the triumph was accepted with joy by Inter owner Massimo Moratti – little wonder after he had waited 11 years to win it. He said, 'I am fully satisfied by the awarding of the title to a club and team that behaved correctly.'

And Mancini was hardly likely to look a gift-horse in the mouth, adding that he and his team deserved it as they had been honest toilers. Roberto said, 'I'm happy. Regardless of how it arrived, it is right to reward those who have given their best and have always been honest. It is strange to win like this but we played fair.'

Some were not as delighted. Inter legend Sandro Mazzola, part of the massively successful Inter side of the 1960s, made it clear he felt this triumph was in no way comparable to those achieved by himself and his team-mates. 'This title can't be compared to the ones that I won, they were different wins in different seasons,' he said. 'Those were other times but now what has happened has happened and there is a league table with Inter in top spot and so it was normal that the award went to Inter. But the fans should be doubly happy - for the title but also because Inter didn't get themselves involved in certain situations.' He was, of course, latterly referring to the fact that Mancini and Inter hadn't fallen foul of the match fixing scandal.

Roberto showed his worth by leading Inter to the title the following season, too, although – once again – the pundits tried to belittle his achievement, pointing out it was inevitably easier with Juve demoted to Serie B and AC Milan suffering from a points deduction.

Mancini merely shrugged his shoulders and got on with the job of winning matches, seemingly oblivious to the catcalls as he led Inter to unprecedented domestic success. Yet he would, surprisingly, only last four seasons at the San Siro because of his failure to deliver on the European stage. He was a victim of his own success: as Moratti held the Serie A title in his hands year after year he began to crave for international recognition. He believed that Mancini should now be delivering the Champions League on a regular basis and he was hardly a patient owner. That led him to seek out Jose Mourinho, who built on Mancini's work and claimed the success in Europe Moratti had demanded – and which Mancini would, arguably, have delivered given more time.

The *Daily Mail* reported on how Moratti delivered the axe to Mancini – despite the success he had brought to the club, 'The 2007/08 campaign ended with another Scudetto it was not without its hiccups as Mancini resigned in the immediate aftermath of the Champions League exit to Liverpool before being swiftly talked into a rethink. And Moratti admitted today that Mancini's apparent willingness to walk out midway through the season had left its mark. Moratti told the *Corriere della Sera* newspaper: "This created imbalances within the team that forced everyone, managers and players included, to double and triple their energies. It's true that we all rowed in the same direction, but we were forced to row harder." Despite the problems which emerged over the final few months of their relationship, Moratti insisted it was not an easy decision to dispense with a coach under whom Inter flourished. He added: "It was not a whim. The most simple solution would have been to have continued with the coach with whom we won three consecutive championships. Nobody would have criticised me, everything would have been smooth. I intervened because I thought it was necessary, not against the coach, but in the interests of Inter." Moratti is expected to name Jose Mourinho as Mancini's replacement. The former Porto and Chelsea boss is likely to take over officially at the start of next week.'

Certainly many Inter fans were enraged by Mancini's dismissal – and the abrupt nature of it. One fan summed up the anger, saying, 'I didn't like the official notice released by Inter, it was a total lack of respect to Mancini. In the end he's been the most winning coach in our history after Helenio Herrera. He deserved to be treated better.'

And that was when Roberto released his own statement, confirming he would be suing for libel, saying the club had damaged his reputation with statements made after his sacking. Mancini's lawyer Stefano Gagliardi released this statement on behalf of his client, 'Inter has misused false and illicit means which have seriously offended my reputation and honour. With reference to the official notice released by Inter this morning, which was diffused and published in all the major Italian and European news agencies and television channels, I have taken the decision to give instructions to my legal team in order to protect my image and reputation against my former employers who used false and illicit means to damage my reputation.

'I would like to thank the president Massimo Moratti and Gabriele Oriali as well as the club and all the staff who have supported me over the last four years. We have to wait and see what the response from Inter will be. I can confirm that we will be taking legal action against the club regarding the statement which was released which has damaged my image.'

More detailed coverage of Roberto's time at Internazionale and his work in bringing Balotelli through the ranks can be found in the earlier chapters on Mario's time at the club – the striker joined Inter in 2006 and flourished under Mancini right from the start of their relationship. Roberto gave him his debut a year later when he was just 17.

Mancini left Inter in 2008 and took time out of the game before joining City in December 2009. He was out of the game for more than 18 months as one of the stipulations of the terms he agreed in a financial deal with Moratti. On paper, Roberto could have been due a pay-off in the region of £10million but in the end was reported to have accepted closer to £3million. It was rumoured he was in contention for the Chelsea job in May 2008 but clearly this was always a no-goer given he still had to agree terms with Moratti and when those terms were rubber-stamped he was forced to sit on the sidelines for a certain period of time.

Eventually, the waiting was over and he would finally end up at Manchester City. Just over seven months after his arrival, Roberto would send for his surrogate son...the stage was set for Mancini and Balotelli to work together again, much to Mario's relief after he had so regularly experienced the rage of Mourinho. He was about to join up once again with the only manager who had ever understood him – and the only man he really felt he could work with in a long-term project. He owed Mancini, for sure – but how would he repay him? We were about to find out...

CHAPTER SIX

WELCOME TO MANCHESTER

As we have pointed out, the writing had been on the wall for Mario at Internazionale for months before he finally left the club and headed for a welcome reunion with Mancini at Man City. Inter boss Mourinho had made it clear he didn't see the boy as having a future at the San Siro as long as he remained manager. Sure, the Portuguese never denied that Mario had the talent needed to become an international superstar – but he also claimed he was 'unmanageable'. Part of the problem was the perennial one when two such strong, self-opinionated characters came together: This town ain't big enough for the both of us.

Mourinho is the type of manager who likes to bask in the limelight and to steal all the publicity, whether bad or good. He does not care for sharing the glory – or the flashes from the paparazzi's lenses. No, he has to be the main man and no player or executive in the club is allowed to step on his ego. That can lead to problems – as he found to his cost with Roman Abramovich at Chelsea. Certainly there could only be one man running that club – and it was never going to be Jose. He found himself sidelined then sacked, much to his shock as Roman let it be known exactly who was boss at Stamford Bridge.

But when he took over at the San Siro he was given total control of team affairs by owner Moratti – and Mourinho was determined to break Balotelli, or get rid of him.

As we have already seen, there would be many incidents of conflict involving the manager and the young striker, but matters started to come to a head during April 2010. Inter beat Barcelona 3-1 in the first leg of their Champions League semi-final clash at the San Siro much to Mourinho's delight. The manager had dreamed of this moment: he had been perpetually irritated that the Barca fans dismissed his achievements in the game and referred to him as 'the interpreter' – a reference to the time he served at the Camp Nou as interpreter to Bobby Robson.

Now his Inter team had taken a crucial step to winning the Champions League with the two-goal lead they would now go to Barcelona with for the second leg. It was Jose's moment – but his limelight would now be stolen by an incident involving Balotelli. The striker was brought on as a sub after 75 minutes and was quickly annoyed by the subdued reaction of the Inter fans to his arrival. He then reacted angrily at full-time, taking off his shirt and throwing it to the ground. Mario, still only 19, had already gestured to the crowd after shooting wide, and now marched angrily towards the tunnel, giving a middle-finger salute to the Inter fans – ruining Mourinho's moment of satisfaction.

After the match then Barcelona striker Zlatan Ibrahimovic claimed that Inter defender Marco Materazzi attacked team-mate Balotelli in the players' tunnel. 'I saw that Materazzi was attacking him in the players' tunnel and I've never seen anything like it,' Ibrahimovic told Italian TV station RAI. 'If I were him, I'd have left Mario alone, but Materazzi was attacking him and I was stunned. If Materazzi had attacked me like that, I would've decked him in a second! Materazzi was causing all sorts of trouble and in the Barcelona locker room we were amazed, all talking about it. A player should be proud after a win, not chase down a youngster to berate him.'

Materazzi wasn't the only employee of Inter angered by Mario's strop. Captain Javier Zanetti said he was 'disappointed that a celebration was ruined with something like this. If the fans whistle at him he's got to understand that it could depend on a lot of different things. We've always stood by him.'

And Dejan Stankovic said: 'He's like a child. I'm a father of three kids and we can't take him by the collar, too. He's suffered, but I've suffered too with the fans. He's reacted poorly, but he's still got time.'

Mourinho himself was far from happy with Balotelli. 'I have been at Inter since July 2008,' he said. 'If I try to remember all the times I've tried to educate a great talent, there are thousands and thousands. This is a Champions League semi-final, the second most important tie in club football, and something ugly happened.'

Inter CEO Ernesto Paolillo promised to clamp down on Mario, telling ESPN, 'Balotelli's gesture was terrible. Just terrible. It is something we are going to have to discuss. Will he be punished? Absolutely, yes.'

Of course Mario was out of order – but it struck me that Mourinho, who had got on his moral high horse over the boy's antics, now had his own tantrum at the post match Press conference as he lashed out at Barcelona, mocking them in defeat! Barca had felt they should have had a penalty but he ridiculed them, pointing out that in the previous year's semi-final his then Chelsea team had had several realistic claims for spot kicks turned down against Barca by (the admittedly hopeless) Norwegian ref Tom Henning Ovrebo. Mourinho scoffed, 'It's a pity. A year ago Chelsea were crying and Barca were laughing with the referee. They laughed because he denied my Chelsea boys their rightful place.'

It would surely have been more appropriate for Mourinho to be generous in victory, but no he could not resist a nasty dig – just minutes after criticising young Mario. But the dispute between Mario and his team-mates that night only served to emphasise the gulf that had developed between them. Mario's days were, clearly, numbered at the San Siro. Surely enough, a couple of weeks later, his agent Mino Raiola confirmed that Mario and Jose had reached the point of no return. Raiola said: 'It's certain that he can't go on like this. Mario won't be staying another year at Inter like this, I can guarantee that. Over the last eight to nine months no one in the club has been protecting Mario.

'Mario is not perfect, just like Mourinho is not horrible. But Mourinho needs a common enemy for himself and the team and Balotelli fell into the trap. Sometimes in training he's even scared. Mario was sure that this would be his year, that he'd be first choice for club and country.'

But Inter Milan were at pains to play down the idea of

Balotelli leaving. Unlike Mourinho, the club's executives truly believed in his talent and wanted him to stay at the club, and by now Rafa Benitez had replaced the Portuguese as boss. Even as late as July 2010, the Inter bosses denied that either Mario or Brazilian full-back Maicon would be sold. The club's technical director Marco Branca said, 'We will consider offers, but they are not transfer listed,' Branca told the Inter website. 'How much is Balotelli worth? He doesn't have a price.'

But he did have a price – and he would be gone before too long…within a month of Branca's denials, in fact.

It was suggested that Mario would now head to England and the Premier League – with many pundits claiming he would end up at the Emirates Stadium given the emphasis Arsenal manager Arsene Wenger always put on players being old enough if they were good enough. And no one, not even Mourinho, had ever denied that Mario wasn't good enough to make it at the very top of the game.

But those who knew Mario better also knew that there could only be one real destination when he left Italy: he would head to Man City to once again link up with his mentor, Mancini. Certainly the fans who had followed Mario's career with interest realised that was going to be the most likely outcome. One supporter said, 'Mancini is like his dad. When they were at Inter together he worked well with Mancini. It's like Bellamy with Mark Hughes – he'll head to Mancini.'

Another fan, Phil, gave an eloquent explanation of why either Mancini or Wenger would be ideal for Balotelli, 'As a Man City fan, I think either my club OR Arsenal would be perfect for Balotelli. The last thing he needs now is to go into a fishbowl existence at Man Utd or Chelsea. Both Mancini and Wenger are just the type to nurture Balotelli and understand that he is a world-beating talent who is going to need some time and space to grow as a footballer and as a person.'

Brilliantly put, Phil. That was just what Mario needed at this stage of his life and career – and he would now get it at City, with Mancini mentoring him once again.

In the second week of August it became clear that Balotelli had only one destination in mind – Mancini and City. The *Guardian* correctly predicted the fee and the salary of the deal, 'Mario Balotelli looks set to complete a £22.5m move from Internazionale to Manchester City in the next 48 hours, having departed Milan for Manchester with his agent Mino Raiola this morning. "We are close with Balotelli," Mancini said. "Hopefully today or tomorrow. Mario is on his way here today." Raiola spent yesterday afternoon in Milan resolving the final details of an agreement with Inter's technical director, Marco Branca, and the club's lawyer Angelo Capellini. Personal terms have already been agreed, and the striker is expected to sign a five-year deal worth €3.5m (£2.875m) a year on completion of a medical at City's training ground today.'

Being Balotelli, he would, naturally, have to sign for the Blues on a date you would remember (or probably would rather not if you were superstitious!) – it was Friday August 13, 2010, that he finally put pen to paper. Unlucky for some, but Mario was overjoyed at the prospect of joining up with the one man who had always stood by him once again.

The *Sun* proclaimed Mario's signing as an exciting one, but, like most newspapers, warned that the boy had an explosive side to his nature too, 'Mario Balotelli has completed his £22million move from Inter Milan to Manchester City. The striker flew into England today to undergo a medical, before signing a five-year deal at Eastlands.

'While Balotelli is one of the hottest prospects in Italian football, he enjoyed a love-hate relationship with former Inter boss Jose Mourinho. It appears the 20-year-old also failed to impress new San Siro chief Rafa Benitez, yet new boss Roberto Mancini – who coached him during their time at Inter – is confident the switch to Eastlands will revitalise the temperamental star.'

City's website, www.mcfc.co.uk officially announced the signing on the 13th, saying, 'Manchester City is delighted to announce that the signing of Mario Balotelli from Inter Milan has been completed for an undisclosed fee. The striker, who celebrated his 20th birthday on Thursday, completed his medical this lunchtime before putting pen to paper on his five-year contract at the City of Manchester Stadium.

'Roberto Mancini, who worked with Mario during his time in charge at the San Siro, said: "I think that Mario is one of the best players of his age in Europe, and I am very happy to be working with him again. His style of play will suit the Premier League, and because he is still so young there is a big chance for him to improve. He is a strong and exciting player, and City fans will enjoy watching him." The Palermo-born frontman faced the Toure brothers during his first senior international appearance earlier this week, but he will not be available for City's first game of the season at White Hart Lane on Saturday.'

Mancini would add more compliments, saying, 'He can play on the wing, as a first striker, a second striker. He's a fantastic player and I genuinely believe in one or two years he will be one of the best players in the world. He's a young guy, just 20 years old, and he has a strong character but he is a good guy, you know. And, most importantly, he is a fantastic footballer. He's just young and, like all young guys, sometimes his behaviour is different, but it's false to say he is not a good man. I've known Mario for three years and I had enough confidence to put him in the first team when he was 17. I have got to know him very well and, OK, sometimes his behaviour is not good, but he is a good man. I think he needs to improve, like a lot of young guys, but I don't think he will have big problems. In England I think Balotelli could be even more of a fantastic player. He can improve here. He is changing country, changing his club, and I think that will be better for him overall.'

On his own website, mariobalotelli.it, Balotelli admitted he would have preferred to stay in Italy, but that he was grateful for the chance to move to England as it would hopefully give him the space and freedom he needed to grow as a player and a person, 'I'm sorry that I'm leaving Inter and Italy because I would have preferred to continue my career in my own country. I'm going where I hope to find the space I need to play which is very important to me: I need to play, to make mistakes, to learn and to play again. As well as a calm environment around me.

'It's been a difficult year. I've recognised my mistakes, but I think I've often been under pressure and on the receiving end of criticism that at times has irritated me. Now all I'm thinking about is playing well for my new club and in the Premier League. I really want to give it my best try! I'd like to thank my family, who have supported me with so much patience and affection, through both the good times and the difficult periods. I also want to thank club chairman Moratti, the team I've shared so many victories with, the fans who've supported me, my entourage and my friends.'

The sentiments shared by Balotelli understandably worried some City fans – that his heart might not be in the City 'project' and that his time and commitment to the club would be fleeting. One City fan said there could be a problem but urged patience, 'He just needs his attitude sorting out, which should be no problem under Mancini at City – most of his problems stemmed from the Inter fans' treatment of him. What do you think turned the Inter fans against him? I would imagine it wouldn't have been for the hell of it. For a young man he seems to have a problem upstairs.'

But another felt the signing was already a big gamble, 'Balotelli is clearly a very talented player, but his temperament and attitude could be a big problem. His interview says it all really. As someone else pointed out he thanked his "entourage", and after joining a new club, in another country, the first thing you say shouldn't be, "I didn't want to leave where I was". Already he doesn't want to be there!'

But yet another fan made the valid point that Balotelli could be 'the business' for City, if he was given a chance – that he had all the necessary attributes to be a big success, even bigger and better than Wayne Rooney, 'When Rooney was 18, he scored 9 in 34 games in the Premier League. When Balotelli was 18, he scored 8 in 22 games whilst playing as a wide forward in Serie A, the most defensive league in the world. Balotelli is strong, quicker, taller and better in the air than Rooney was at his age, and to top it off is a very good set-piece taker. Even as an English football fan, there is no doubt that Balotelli has the potential to be better than Rooney. It's just typical English bias if you think otherwise.'

Another backer of Balotelli was a City fan in Sydney, Australia, who said, 'To me, this signing trumps them all. Robinho, Carlos Tevez, David Silva...the lot. A kid, who by the age of 20, has three Serie A titles, a Champions League medal, and the footballing world at his feet. He could very well be our Cristiano Ronaldo, or at the very least, our Wayne Rooney. Very, very happy days indeed.'

Certainly City defender Kolo Toure believed that Balotelli would be a huge success at City. The Ivory Coast star had faced Mario in an international match against Italy, just before Balotelli joined the Blues – and admitted he had been a handful to keep in check. Toure said, 'He is perfect for the English game. He reminds me of Roy Keane and Patrick Vieira, these type of guys. They have a really strong mentality and, in the Premier League, we like those kind of players.'

Even then Chelsea boss Carlo Ancelotti felt Balotelli would run riot in the Premier League, having witnessed his development while manager at AC Milan. Ancelotti said, 'Mario is a crazy talent. With him Manchester City will challenge for the title, not just fourth. England is ideal for him. There is too much pressure on young players in Italy, and there is almost no racism to contend with in England.'

Mancini had no doubts about Balotelli's ability and potential to make it big in England. He showed just how much he rated Mario by immediately dropping Roque Santa Cruz from City's Europa League squad so that he could instead accommodate Balotelli in it. The manager had taken advantage of a rule that permitted clubs to make one late change to their original squad for the knockout round – and Balotelli benefited by immediately being parachuted in. It showed just how much Mancini rated him – that he would toss aside a proven international in Santa Cruz for him.

Mancini would now throw Mario in for his debut in the Europa League knockout stage first-leg match against FC Timisoara. Before the game Mario was at pains to claim that he was not 'the bad boy' the likes of Mourinho had claimed him to be. He said, 'I am not a bad boy. They say this in Italy, but I am just a normal guy. I really don't know why I have a reputation as a "bad boy", but I don't care about it. And as for Mourinho, he is not my coach now and I don't want to talk about him. The reason I wanted to be here at City was because of the manager and because it is a good environment for me to improve.'

Balotelli admitted that the racist chanting at grounds in Italy had 'hurt him' and that he wanted to move to England to be with Mancini, but also to get away from that abuse. He was aware that racial abuse at grounds in England was a thing of the past and that the country was a much more multicultural one than Italy. He said he was 'concerned' that he might suffer abuse from the terraces in Romania – where racism in football was still not under control – but that that prospect would not stop him making his debut for City, or, hopefully, enjoying it too.

Mario said, 'I just want to play. I'm not thinking about what might happen. Racism is something that has really bothered me but I've learned how to deal with it, by pretending that it doesn't hurt. As far as I know there is no racism in English football. There were two or three incidents in Italy. I hope I don't have them again.'

Well, Mario would get off to a flier in the Europa League clash in Romania. City had been struggling to break down a dogged and determined FC Timisoara and Mancini decided to bring on Balotelli just before the hour mark in an attempt to shake things up and hopefully add an injection of urgency to proceedings. The move worked a treat – within 15 minutes of emerging, Mario had scored the goal that would divide the two clubs, earning City a 1-0 win on the night and sending them home confident they would put the tie to bed in the return leg in Manchester.

The only downside was when the young Italian striker picked up a knock in injury-time. He had scored and got injured on his debut – typical Mario, as they say back in Italy, never goes quietly into any situation! Mancini was delighted with his boy's debut showing, saying, 'He had a great debut. I am happy he scored. He's a good player. He needs to improve of course and get to know everybody. It was the first time he had played with the team. We must work on this with him because it will be different in the Premier League than in Italy.'

Of his injury, Mancini added, 'We do not think it is serious. It was probably just a kick, it is not a problem. It was a difficult game for us because Timisoara are a good team and they played very well in the first half. In the end, it is a good result for us. But they made it difficult for us by getting so many players behind the ball. All the players played well, especially in the second half and we moved the ball quickly. I think we deserved to score another goal because we had three or four good chances.'

The media were impressed. They now realised that City

had bought a powerhouse of a footballer – as well as a controversial one. The *Mail*'s Colin Young said, 'So this is what all the fuss was about, then. In the space of 15 minutes Mario Balotelli nearly grabbed a hat-trick, escaped a booking, got two lectures from the referee, did earn one yellow card, squared up to the opposition captain and needed treatment from the medics in injury time.

'Oh, and he scored the winner. Audiences back home were denied the chance to see the 20-year-old's City debut, but on this evidence, they will be in for a treat when he is unleashed on the Barclays Premier League.'

Meanwhile, the *Sun*'s Martin Blackburn also made the point that City fans had surely now found a new hero to worship – a hero and an undoubted showman who could light up even the dullest of games. Blackburn said, 'Keep your eyes on Mario Balotelli – he's going to be great box office at Manchester City. The 20-year-old so-called bad boy of Italian football showed both sides of his character just days after joining from Inter Milan. It is difficult to imagine a more explosive debut than the 33-minute cameo he made here in Romania. He spared City's blushes by slamming in an Emmanuel Adebayor cross to finally break down stubborn Timisoara just 15 minutes after coming on.

'But he also picked up a yellow card for squaring up to an opponent – and could have had another for flattening a defender while going for a header. Then he went agonisingly close on two occasions before ending the night with lengthy treatment after being clattered late on. One thing's for sure, it won't be dull at Eastlands with him around. And we were all grateful as he brought this Europa League play-off tie to life after 57 minutes of boredom.'

City's official website were also purring over Mario's debut, 'Mario Balotelli lived up to his "Super Mario" nickname with an explosive cameo off the subs bench in Timisoara this evening. The powerful former Inter Milan striker scored the only goal in City's 1-0 win over their Romanian opponents to take help the Blues take a huge step towards the group stages of the Europa League ahead of next week's return in Manchester. Balotelli stroked home the winner on 71 minutes after great work by Yaya Toure and Emmanuel Adebayor. If this is a taste of things to come, the City fans may have just found a new hero.'

Mario himself was just as pleased with his 33-minute cameo debut in Romania and promised City fans there was much more to come from him. Balotelli said: 'I feel good, this is the kind of debut I dreamed of. I showed up for Manchester City immediately and I will continue to show up for them. These are only the first games we are playing together but we will get better and better. My right leg aches a bit. I think it may be a cartilage thing, the problem is I do not have much muscle there. It's a bit of a problem, but I'm sure I will be available against Liverpool.'

He really did want to make his Premier League debut against Liverpool the following Monday night. It was the night that the club's owner Sheikh Mansour would make his first visit to Eastlands to watch the team. But it was not to be: the injury was worse than expected and kept him on the sidelines, although the Sheikh was still delighted by what he saw as City ran out 3-0 winners.

Before the match, Mancini had once again bigged up Mario, saying he had the potential to be a better striker than Liverpool's then centre-forward Fernando Torres and had the world at his feet. Roberto said, 'Balotelli could be as good as Torres and even better. Torres can only play as a striker, Balotelli can play as striker and a winger. He has a different attitude. What is sure is that we are talking about two fantastic players. The defenders do not know much about Mario, but they will see he can change everything about a game. I saw him four years ago when I was at Inter Milan. He was 16 or 17. It was the last five games of the Serie A championship. We had Ibrahimovic injured and we played Mario inside and he played like someone who was 30 years old. That's because he has good technique, he has everything.'

It was some billing for the new young striker – now City fans were impatient to see him in action in England. They wouldn't have to wait long...

CHAPTER SEVEN

BOY BLUE

Mario was eager to show City fans just what he was capable of after scoring on his debut in the Europa League clash in Romania. But the 'knock' he had suffered against FC Timisoara would prove to be substantially more than that – and he would now be sidelined for just over two months.

It was a big setback for the Italian – like most competitive players he hated sitting around on the sidelines and found it tough going as he worked on a programme of rehabilitation. The 'knock' proved to be a bad injury to the lateral meniscus in his right knee – an injury that would require surgery and put him out of action until the end of October 2010.

City announced on 8 September that the knee would need surgery after attempts to let the injury clear up itself with rest and physio failed. Goal.com and BBC Sport were the first to reveal the setback. Goal said, '[Balotelli's] hope of making his home debut for Manchester City on Saturday against Blackburn have been dashed after the club confirmed that he will undergo knee surgery that will keep him out of action for "up to six weeks". The striker picked up the injury in City's Europa League win over FC Timisoara on August 19, a game in which Balotelli scored just 15 minutes after coming off the bench. With key Premier League games against Chelsea and Arsenal coming up for City, the club had hoped that surgery wouldn't be needed to solve the problem, but they have now confirmed that it was the only option.'

While the BBC added, '...despite undergoing a rest period since in a bid to cure the problem, the club decided to operate after a setback in training this week. The Italian will therefore miss City's Premier League match against Chelsea and a Europa League tie with Juventus. Balotelli signed from Inter Milan in the summer for £21m but has played only 33 minutes for the club so far - as a second-half substitute in City's 1-0 Europa League win over Romanian side Timisoara last month.'

The club confirmed the situation, saying, 'Striker Mario Balotelli is to undergo surgery on his injured knee that could rule him out for up to six weeks. Roberto Mancini's summer capture from Inter has flown back to Milan with key Barclays Premier League clashes against champions Chelsea and top-four rivals Arsenal looming at City of Manchester Stadium.

'Balotelli, who damaged the knee during his scoring debut against Timisoara in Romania last month, will also miss the Europa League group home game against his old rivals Juventus. The Italian's injury is to the lateral meniscus, one of the two most crucial structures in the knee, and medical wisdom is to try and encourage the problem to heal without recourse to an operation.

'It was hoped that the symptoms would settle down but once Balotelli began to step up his recovery programme this week, it became clear that action would need to be taken.'

Some City fans now voiced fears that Balotelli had been a waste of money; that he was injury-prone, temperamental (as exhibited by his booking in Romania when he clashed with one of their players) and that he was only using Manchester as an indirect route to make it back to Milan. That he actually wanted to play for AC Milan but knew Inter would not sell him directly – so he was using City as a staging-post to AC Milan. But other fans rushed to reassure the doubters. One said, 'Easily your best signing chaps. I've seen him play plenty in Serie A and he has everything. Blistering pace, wonderful technique (both shooting and delivery) and physical strength. I can't say I enjoy City buying lots of high profile players, and do believe some have been rushed, expensive and unnecessary (Silva maybe, Kolarov) but this guy can take you to the next level.

'If you throw in Yaya and Milner, along with existing players Tevez and Kompany, and providing you can keep hold of them all, you have 5 plus positions that are covered for another 5-7 years or more. Best of luck to Super Mario, from a football fan's point of view I'm itching to see him light up the Prem.'

While another added, 'In every generation of footballers there are a few elite players that will outshine the rest. But out of these few elite superstars only one will be remembered as one of the greatest of all time. And out of these all-time-greats only one will have the berth bestowed on him as the greatest player to have ever graced the football pitch. This man will be Super Mario Balotelli.'

My sources confirmed that Mario WAS committed to City and had no intention of cutting loose early and heading back to Milan. 'OK, one day he would for sure like to play for AC,' I was told, 'but that would be one day far in the future. His friends and family were back in Milan and Italy so it is inevitable that he will return one day. But not for some years – his intention was to stay at City for a few years and learn and grow as a person and a footballer.

'He knew he had to escape the goldfish bowl of Italian football and he had no wish to go back until the racism issue was sorted...which could take many years. It was certainly NOT the case that he wanted to go back as soon as he had got to Manchester. He wanted to show the City fans what he could do and he wanted to repay Mancini for having the faith to pay so much money for him. He was gutted that he got injured so early in his City career and his only aim was to get fit again and do the business for the fans who were clearly so keen to see him in action. I would say there was little chance of him leaving City for some years – certainly not unless Mancini headed off into the sunset. That might change his view, but he wanted to stay and play.'

The Associated Press reported that Mario's operation had gone well. He had returned to Italy for it so that he could convalesce with friends and family. AP announced on Thursday September 9, 'Manchester City striker Mario Balotelli has undergone successful surgery on a right knee injury that is expected to keep him out for about six weeks. The 20-year-old striker waved to reporters from his window at the San Matteo hospital in Pavia, Italy, on Thursday, shirtless but wearing a shower cap. Earlier, surgeons took 20 minutes to remove part of the lateral meniscus on his right knee, which he tore in a Europa League match against FC Timisoara last month. Balotelli scored the winner in that game, his debut for City after he joined for 22.5 million pounds ($35 million) from Inter Milan.'

His convalescence began a couple of days after the op, when he left the hospital – and the first thing he stressed as he limped away was how keen he was to play for City. As the Mail reported, 'Mario Balotelli is desperate to pull on a Manchester City shirt again following a successful operation on his injured knee. His recovery is expected to take around six weeks but the 20-year-old was staying positive as he left the San Matteo hospital in Pavia, Italy. "I'm fine and the surgery went well," he told corrieredellosport.it. "I hope to return to play in as little time as possible."'

Not the most patient of men, Mario nonetheless allowed himself some healing time after the operation. By the end of September, 2010, the knee had improved dramatically and he was ready to begin light training. On 30 September, Mancini said, 'He is (still) in Italy today and his knee is okay. I think he may be ready at the end of October.' If the prognosis proved correct, Balotelli would be available for City's home clash against fellow Premier League title hopefuls Arsenal. That match would take place in Manchester on Sunday 24 October and a few days beforehand Mancini gave Mario a major boost by naming him in the squad for the game.

He had trained with his team-mates during the week before the crunch title clash and was expected to make the subs' bench if there were no further setbacks to the knee.

Mario did make the bench for the match, and came on as a sub for his home debut after 72 minutes, replacing Gareth Barry. But it would not be a home debut he would want to remember as City crashed 3-0 to the Gunners.

City had been up against it from just five minutes in when Dedryck Boyata was sent off for bringing down Marouane Chamakh when he was the last defender. The Blues were 2-0 down when Mario appeared and he was unable to turn things around. Understandably he was a little rusty having been out of action for so long. He found it difficult to impose himself on the game and Arsenal went on to score again, through a late Nicklas Bendtner goal.

Mancini was, understandably, depressed by the result but was still optimistic about the future – and was convinced that Mario would help bring about a better future at City. He declared himself 'pleased' that Mario had come back from injury without any further setbacks and added, 'I think against Arsenal it is difficult to play 11 versus 11. Ten against 11 is worse but it is my opinion that we if played 11 against 11 we would have won this game. I am very proud of my players because I think they played very well. They tried always to score, always to defend very well. I think they showed we are one of the best teams in the Premier League.'

Mario had been at City for more than two months but had yet to make his full debut for the club after suffering that injury blow in Romania. But now he was finally reaching peak fitness and was ready to roll – much to his and Mancini's relief.

'He was just glad to get through the Arsenal match without aggravating the injury,' I was told. 'Of course the result was a disappointment and he would have liked to have done more to impress the fans – but he knew his time would come. His aim was to be fully fit and then he would show how good he was.'

The chance came sooner than he had expected. Mancini took him aside a couple of days before City's match and told Mario that he would finally be in the starting line-up for the club. The landmark occasion would be against Wolverhampton Wanderers at Molineux and Mario was suitably excited at the prospect. 'He wasn't nervous,' I was told, 'he doesn't really get affected by nerves. But he was really looking forward to it – it had been a long time coming and now he was determined to go out there and make an impact.'

But it didn't quite work out how Mario would have liked. For the second game in a row he and City were on the wrong end of a defeat, this time unexpectedly losing 2-1 as Wolves belied their status as one of the favourites for relegation from the Premier League. Mario admitted the match was 'frustrating' for him with only a yellow card to commemorate his big day in English football – and few signs of the talent and technique that had persuaded Mancini to fork out a fortune for his services. Mario had taken the place of the injured Tevez in the team, but it was a full debut he would want to forget – as Paul Jiggins of the *Sun* pointed out, 'Tevez's absence meant Mario Balotelli was finally handed his full debut following his arrival from Inter in August. Before Saturday, the only impression the 6ft 3in striker had made in Manchester was on the BMW he collided with while at the wheel of his Audi. Well, after his debut he can now say he has been involved in two car crashes since joining City.

'Balotelli, like his team-mates, faded badly after Emmanuel Adebayor fired them ahead with a 23rd-minute penalty following Richard Stearman's foul on David Silva. But, after Serbian midfielder Nenad Milijas levelled with a left-footed shot from the edge of the area seven minutes later, Mancini's men rolled over in pathetic fashion.'

Afterwards Mario would admit he found it hard going – but vowed that he would come good and show the potential that marked him down as one of the future greats of football. 'It was difficult for me on Saturday because it was my first full game after all the injuries,' Balotelli said before heading to Poland for the Europa League game with Poznan. 'The tackles are harder and the referees don't seem to blow very often for fouls – in Italy, when someone makes contact with you, it's a foul, but that's not the case in England.

'It was my first game and it wasn't easy for me because I need to get to know my team-mates on the pitch and understand their movement and that comes with time.

'I want to be the best player in the world. It is good to have ambition. I've said in the past that I don't care what other people want or expect of me because I know what I want, I will always give everything because I want to become the best. That is my aim and I am determined to make it happen. I am here at City to play Champions League football, that's the competition I want to be in and that is what all the players here want to play in.'

Mancini was angry with all his big-name stars after such a dire showing – Mario included, although he did give his fellow Italian some leeway on account of him still recovering from that lengthy spell out on the sidelines injured. Roberto

Above left: Balotelli celebrates scoring a goal against Atalanta at the Atleti Azzurri d'Italia stadium, 2008.

Above right: Balotelli charging for possession of the ball against Germany's Ashkan Dejagah, Italy v Germany 2009.

Below left: Balotelli points to the star emblem on his club shirt after scoring a second goal for his team. Inter Milan v Siena 2009.

Below right: Coach Jose Mourinho discussing game tactics with Balotelli, Inter Milan v Palermo 2009.

Above: Balotelli looks on during fixtures against Bologna, 2009.

Below: Balotelli bypassing Atalanta goalkeeper Ferdinando Coppola to score his second goal of the match.

Above: Balotelli holding the cup trophy after Inter Milan claim their fifth consecutive Serie A title in 2010.

Below: Balotelli celebrating victory over Bayern Munich with fans in 2010.

Above: Balotelli and fellow Inter Milan teammates attend Pope Benedict XVI's weekly general audience in Saint Peter's Square, 2008.

Below: Italy v Sweden in 2009 at Olympia Stadium, Helsingborg, Sweden.

Above: Balotelli defends Germany's Andres Breck's attempt on the ball, Italy v Germany 2009.

Below: Brotherly love – Leonardo Bonucci (*left*), Balotelli and Antonio Cassano (*right*).

Above: Inter Milan defeat AS Roma to win the Italian Cup, 2010.

Below left: Manchester City manager poses with the newly signed Balotelli at the club's Carrington training complex in Manchester, England, 2010.

Below right: AS Roma's Simone Perrotta (*left*) attempts to intercept Balotelli's charge for the goal.

Above: Inter Milan players Diago Milito (*left*) and Goran Pandev (*right*) congratulate Balotelli for scoring another goal during their 2010 match against Bologna.

Below left: Balotelli with Marco Matgrazzi during their Champions League match against Rubin Kazan, 2009.

Below right: Balotelli practises strikes at a training session, 2009.

Snapshot during training at Cracovia Stadium, Krakow, Poland in 2009.

could be seen throwing off some of his clothes the angrier he became and he later admitted, 'I took off my coat, scarf and tie because I was hot and because I was angry. I thought it was impossible for us to play like we did in the second half. The second half is the worst we have played since I came here. I have to speak to my players to try to understand why we played like this.

'But if we can understand why we lost this game and we get back to playing like we did one week ago, then the season is very long – and everything can change in football.'

Mario would finally truly announce himself on the English stage just a week later when he started for City for the second time, away at West Brom. This time it would be a match he and the fans would never forget...for good and bad reasons! Balotelli would score both goals as the Blues won 2-0, but get sent off just after the hour mark. The *Sun*'s Steven Howard eloquently summed up the crazy scenario, saying, 'Yesterday we had Mario Balotelli's first league goals for City since his move from Inter Milan – scored in a seven-minute spell in the first half. The first came when he extended a telescopic leg – the left one on this occasion – to convert a Carlos Tevez cross at the far post in the 20th minute while the second saw him muscle Gabriel Tamas off the ball before shooting across Scott Carson.

'Being Balotelli, though, it didn't end there. The boy who came with a reputation of having an attitude problem – and loves nothing better than a pose, a pout or, preferably, a scowl for no good reason – couldn't leave it at that. He had himself sent off in only his fourth game for the club. Yes, there was some sympathy for the hot-headed Italian since the incident with Youssouf Mulumbu that saw him dismissed in the 62nd minute was hardly worth a yellow card let alone the straight red produced by Lee Probert.

'You can only imagine Probert thought Balotelli had followed his challenge with a boot in the prone Mulumbu's stomach though TV evidence proved this not to be the case. Yet Balotelli was asking for trouble by getting involved in anything borderline 60 seconds after picking up a yellow for dissent after a comical attempt at winning a penalty.'

Mancini claimed the red was unwarranted but that didn't stop him having a go at Mario for getting sent off as he walked from the pitch. He said, 'I absolutely do not agree with the referee about this sending off. A red card for what? Mario played a fantastic game, he scored two goals, but the sending off was very strange.

'I want to know why it was a direct red card. For me this is not correct and the referee must explain. I am angry because I explained to Mario before the game, pay attention with the referee. I wanted to change Adam Johnson for Mario but I didn't have time to make the change.'

Roberto insisted that the club appeal against the sending off – but the FA refused to budge on the decision which meant that Mario would now miss out on the club's next match...what would have been his first derby match against Manchester United...plus the visit of Birmingham and a trip to Fulham. An FA statement said: 'At a Regulatory Commission hearing today, a claim that the standard punishment is clearly excessive from Manchester City's Mario Balotelli was dismissed. As a result, Balotelli will serve a three match suspension with immediate effect.'

Mario would now miss three weeks of football. It was an unsatisfactory situation: he had already been sidelined for two months with injury, now lack of discipline had cost him more time twiddling his thumbs on the sidelines. By the end of November 2010, he had been at City for 16 weeks but had been out of action for 11 weeks.

He made his comeback on 27 November in a difficult looking encounter at Stoke. The fans at the Britannia Stadium were among the most vocal in the Premier League and the team were known as 'the dogs of war' because of their physical approach: it was thus a high-profile return and Mancini told Mario he would have to be extra careful not to be riled by the crowd or the opposition. Roberto knew he would find it hard to defend his boy if he suffered another red card.

Micah Richards had put City ahead but Stoke denied them all three points when Matt Etherington equalised, much to the disappointment of Mancini who was celebrating his 46th birthday that Saturday.

Mario certainly did not appear to be in the mood for a tough battle. Appearing with a snood and gloves he looked as though he would rather be somewhere warmer and did not put in the shift the fans or his manager would have expected.

But Micah rushed to defend his new team-mate, saying, 'It was hard for Mario. He probably hasn't been anywhere like this before and the crowd were giving him some stick. He may have to get used to that, but technically he's a genius. At places like this, defenders might want to smash him from behind, but I thought he coped well and there's a lot more to come from him.'

'But this is probably the sort of place we need to come and win at if we're serious about winning the title.'

I was told by a City source that, 'Yes, Mario didn't enjoy

the trip to the Britannia. He was annoyed by the abuse he received from the Stoke crowd and struggled to get into the game. He was also a bit fearful of getting involved in any incidents that could lead to bookings or trouble with the ref. If you take away all his aggression and commitment, you don't have the same player.'

It's a fair comment. It is the same for the majority of footballing greats...or would-be greats like Mario. Even Lionel Messi has his moments of defiance and anger underneath that little-boy façade.

Yet the following Wednesday it would be a different Balotelli on show – the one who can cause chaos in any defence when he is in the mood – as he grabbed a brace against Salzburg to propel City into the last 32 of the Europa League. It was Mario who opened the scoring in the first half with a finely judged volley and he grabbed his second with an easy tap-in during the second half. A goal by Adam Johnson confirmed City's arrival in the last 32.

Afterwards Mancini admitted he was happy with Balotelli's brace but, ever the perfectionist, added that he still expected more from the boy – and that he should be demanding more of himself. Mancini said, 'He's a good striker but he must improve. He can play better than he did tonight. He's always like this because it is normal for him to score. I am happy he scored but he can do more. He didn't smile or celebrate, but he's always like this. Maybe if he'd been fit for the season he could have got us an extra couple of points.

'But I'm happy with qualification – we can now focus on the Premier League. We could have had a better result had we converted our three or four chances in the first half.'

The local paper, the *Manchester Evening News*, was left purring by Mario's display and the whole enigmatic presence of the man, saying, 'Balotelli plays his football as if he is having a lazy afternoon knock about with pals on one of the sunny beaches in his native Palermo.

'His effortless style can sometimes be infuriating amid the rigours of English football, but on nights like this it just places him a class above the opposition – and most of his team-mates.

'His goals helped to extend the Blues' unbeaten run to six games, their best run since Roberto Mancini took the reins nearly a year ago.'

The *Mail* focused on the talent and box office appeal of Balotelli, saying, 'A night that offered another fascinating insight into the enigmatic Italian. Balotelli is certainly good box office.'

That description enraged some football fans. One, Peter Giannis, of Cyprus, commented, 'There is nothing fascinating, enigmatic or good box office about Balotelli. Just a dysfunctional, ill-mannered, attention seeking, astronomically paid petulant mercenary and to paint him otherwise is plain misleading! The real star last night that was pure box office and a joy to watch was...Adam Johnson! He scored a great individual goal and he actually celebrated it! He also happens to be English which can only be good for the England team.'

To which City fans naturally enough disagreed. One summed up the mood of the diehard Blues, pointing out, 'Well he's got your attention enough for you to actually take the time out to write a little letter about him?? He's not your typical over the top celebrator of goals like some...'

That was the essence of Mario: he could infuriate or leave you drooling. You either loved him or hated him: there was no in-between, no grey area – always the characteristics one would associate with the great mavericks of the game over the years. Whether it be George Best, Paul Gascoigne or Eric Cantona.

Other City fans were eager to voice their delight at the devastation their maverick Italian had caused. One said, 'Well now I'm more convinced than ever that Mancini is the man. I say that because he managed to talk a player like Mario Balotelli in to coming to play for us. This is just the start of things to come for Mario. He will turn into the world's best player and we will bask in a blaze of glory because of it. I'm not over the top at all, I just know it.'

While another said, 'I'll go to bed a bit happier tonight having seen our largely second eleven ease to victory without finding third gear. How cool was Signor Mario Balotelli's first! The more you see that goal the more it reveals about the kid - mentally he is clearly a few moves ahead of the other mere mortals around him which is where the calm comes from. He is going to be the terror of defences worldwide, I just can't wait for the next game against the trotters. Blue Moon rising or what!'

And another added, 'Balotelli...Showing the talent that makes him what he is already. World Class. Before he joined us he was already the hottest young property in Italy and now at last, in Britain we can see it for ourselves. We have a superstar. He can score goals for fun and it is very easy for him. Other deluded clubs talk about the talented kids they have. What a joke. This guy is the real deal.'

And another City fan predicted Balotelli would have Man

United quaking come the next derby day encounter, 'Balotelli…is pure class not just in his play but how he just makes the statement, "I will do it in my time not yours." This lad knows how good he is and he gets a kick out of winding people up the wrong way – not just his own team-mates but other players and officials. He will get right under Sir Purple Nose's skin for sure role on derby day!'

'Mario was really pleased that the fans had finally caught a real glimpse of just what he could offer – and that they were delighted with him,' I was told. 'He hadn't enjoyed the cold weather – as you could probably tell by his body language! – but the warmth of the fans and his team-mates made up for it all. He felt at home – that he had laid down something of a marker and that he could now build upon it. He really wanted to work on a relationship with the fans…that was what he missed out on at Internazionale. He is a player who needs to be loved – and the Salzburg match was, he hoped, the start of his love-in with the City supporters.'

It was the start of December, 2010, and Mario would now go on to make another five appearances before the New Year. He and City would win four of those five Premier League games – beating Bolton at home 1-0, West Ham away 3-1, Newcastle away 3-1 and Aston Villa at home 4-0. They would lose at home to Everton 2-1 in between the West Ham and Newcastle clashes.

Mario would not score in the first four games – he would play his part in the victories but would only earn two yellow cards (against West Ham and Newcastle) before the final match of the year at home to Villa.

But he would be the star of the show and snatch all the

headlines as City saw out the old year with a stunning show – and he grabbed his first hat-trick for the club with a scintillating personal display. The win even sent City to the top of the league – although it was only temporary as neighbours United would regain top spot in a later game that day.

Mario's opener was his first in the league at home for the club and relieved some of the pressure that seemed to have been building on him. With it being the festive season he had, naturally enough, been feeling slightly homesick – but the hat-trick and the good wishes of his new fans helped put the smile back on his face.

BBC Sport summed up his performance, saying, 'Mario Balotelli scored a hat-trick as Manchester City secured an emphatic victory over out-of-form Aston Villa. Balotelli struck from the penalty spot after Eric Lichaj had fouled him before Joleon Lescott headed in City's second. Balotelli tapped in a rebound before scoring with a second spot-kick after Marc Albrighton tripped Adam Johnson...The 20-year-old Italian had only mustered two Premier League goals prior to Tuesday's contest but he showed that he can provide a potent alternative to Carlos Tevez, who was on the bench as he rested a sore hamstring, in the lone striker role.'

Afterwards Mancini admitted that Mario was suffering from being away from his family and friends at Christmas and New Year – but stressed he felt the boy would overcome the problem and that he wanted him to stay and become one of the best players on the planet. Mancini said: 'Maybe he is homesick but I don't think it's a long-term problem. He is 20, has left his family for the first time – it's normal to miss them. It is very important to keep him. He is a very good player and he can improve a lot. I think it is very important for the guys to help Mario. This season is a very important experience for him.

'If he plays like he did today he can be one of the top players in Europe.'

Mario had scored eight goals in 11 games – a more than creditable return – but some pundits and fans were concerned that he rarely seemed to celebrate the goals. They felt it showed he was not committed to the club and the country, although Mario denied this. He said it was just his way – and Mancini backed up that claim, pointing out that he had rarely gone over the top when he scored for Inter.

Mario himself said, 'I am happy even if journalists keep saying that I want to leave and go back to Milan. I am always happy, even when I don't smile. I feel a striker has to score. It is my job. That is why I don't smile.

'I am here and I am working hard in training. I want to be an important man for this team and the results are on the pitch. We can win this championship. In the new year we can be better.'

City fans were certainly keen for Mario to stay and continue to prove himself after the show against Villa. One City fan said, 'He is a very young and talented lad with a huge potential – which I hope Mancini can get him to build on. He has scored a hat-trick today which may have included two penalties - but that still takes bottle and he hasn't got out of second gear!'

And even non Blues supporters were full of admiration for Mario's show against Villa – and pointed out it was not that easy when you were adapting to life in a new country. One footie fan said, 'Twenty years old in a different country without his family, of course he would be miserable and homesick. Eight goals already – I would take a miserable 20 year old like Balotelli anytime. Just imagine if he settles down over here in a year's time or two. Those who are saying his attitude is terrible or are criticising him personally are obviously not aware of his circumstances.

'I do not support any English team so am impartial. Balotelli is an incredibly talented footballer who has had to go through a hell of a lot in his short life. He was adopted and his relationship with his birth parents is positively toxic. He had to grow up with deplorable racist abuse when he played and had to cope with this complicated family situation all under the spotlight of being one of the most talented young footballers on the planet.

'I wonder how those criticising him would have coped living abroad at 20 – on your own, being hounded in the Press and told you have an attitude problem. I think he's coping remarkably well considering what he has been through. Dealing with fame and money at a very young age is difficult, and he clearly isn't the most educated guy. Great player and I hope he is able to fulfil his talent - he's had to be a fighter to get this far.'

And a Chelsea fan added, 'He will be one of the best players in the world. I would have loved for him to join us. I have a lot of respect for Man City and I hope the fans enjoy the success that money will bring. Just brush off fans of other clubs that criticise the fact that success will arrive in this way. Who cares? I wish Abramovich would get spending again...'

It was a fair comment and Balotelli was certainly feeling less homesick, and more contented, after that hat-trick – his final act of his first half of his first season in England. Not a bad way to see out the old year – and see in the new. 'Mario was much happier after that,' I was told, 'It settled him down, he had been pining to return home for Christmas and it had been very tough for him – he was, after all, a young lad away from his family – and at Christmas time. But now he was looking forward to the second half of the season. He knew the City fans loved him and that all he had to do was keep hitting the back of the net and things would continue to get better. Yes, that first hat-trick couldn't have come at a better time...'

Now all he needed to do was keep up the good work in 2011.

CHAPTER EIGHT

GOLDEN YEAR

Mario ended 2010 and started 2011 in his usual style – surrounded by controversy! He was headline news in all the tabloids when he won the 'Golden Boy' award. The honour is bestowed upon the player deemed the best young footballer in Europe.

It is a prestigious award, organised by the Turin newspaper *Tuttosport* and voted for by European journalists in recognition of the player they rate as the most talented under 21-year-old on the Continent. But rather than just accepting it with grace and gratitude, Mario typically put his foot in it by unwittingly dropping a clanger. The *Sun* described his faux pas as 'provocative' – and other papers were equally damning. It all flared up when Mario was asked what he thought about second place Arsenal midfielder Jack Wilshere. He replied: "What's his name? Wil...? No, I don't know him, but the next time I play against Arsenal I will keep a close eye on him. Perhaps I can show him the Golden Boy trophy and remind him that I won it."'

It was a classic putdown but, I am told, he genuinely didn't know Wilshere by name – although he later recognised him when he was shown a picture!

Mario then managed to knock Cesc Fabregas, Wayne Rooney and Rafael van der Vaart, all of whom had also previously won the award. He said none of them were as good as him! Mario added, 'There's only one that is a little stronger than me: Messi. All the others are behind me. I am delighted to receive the award, but who should have won it but me? Two years ago I finished sixth and then fourth in 2009. It was finally my turn. My aim is that this prize will transform itself into the Ballon d'Or. To have won this award is a good omen to achieve that. 'For 2011 I want the Premier League, in order to continue with the tradition I had at Inter of winning three consecutive titles, and to clinch the Europa League, a trophy I have not yet won and a competition where we are considered favourites.'

It all led one writer, Chris Wright, to describe Mario as 'utterly myopic, self-centred, self-interested, alienating, egotistical, petulant, ridiculously immature, head-strong, off-puttingly pugnacious, cripplingly arrogant, impudent and as having no decisive measure of his footballing worth other than his ridiculously inflated salary'. To which a City fan replied, 'So exactly like 90 per cent of players in the Premiership, then? Except he doesn't pretend otherwise, which I kinda like in the guy – come on, who else hates all that, "it's an honour just to be nominated alongside such wonderful... crap?'

At least Mario was set to start the New Year with a bang on the field. Well, he had netted that wonderful hat-trick against Villa at the end of 2010, hadn't he? But, as with most things concerned with Balotelli, nothing was that simple. Just as he had found the sort of form that Mancini had promised he was capable of regularly delivering, Mario suffered another setback.

Early in January 2011, City announced that he had suffered another injury – that would keep him out of action for at least a month. Of course, he had already been sidelined for many weeks earlier in the campaign with a knee problem and a suspension for his red card.

It left Mancini tearing his hair out. Initially, he believed it would just sideline Mario for a few days – at the same time as David Silva also suffered an injury. Roberto said, 'It is a big problem. Neither of them will be available. David has been an important player for us and has been doing well recently. Hopefully, he will be back for the Wolves game on 15 January. Mario might be back for the FA Cup tie at Leicester on Sunday.'

At the time City were joint top of the table with United but Mancini was keen to play down their chances as they had completed two more games than their neighbours. He added, 'Arsenal, Chelsea, United and Tottenham all have more experience than us. Probably one of those four teams will win the title. We just want to work, so we can improve and try to keep getting better.'

His mood became even more pessimistic when he then learned that Mario would be out for far longer than a couple of days. He said, 'I'm worried because he can't play for another three or four weeks at an important moment for us. To have an operation done and then to have another problem two months later is strange. He may need surgery. We just don't know. He must rest, then he will have treatment and work. Hopefully then he will be OK.'

At least Mancini had a £27million fallback option in the form of Edin Dzeko, whom he had just signed from Wolfsburg in Germany. The big Bosnian striker would go straight into the team for the next Premier League match while forlorn Mario now faced a further six-week lay-off.

At the end of January, Mancini decided it was time to try to sort Mario's knee problem once and for all, by sending him to a top specialist in America, who had helped rugby ace Jonny Wilkinson continue to play after a serious knee injury. The *Independent* reported that Roberto had 'put him in the care of the world-renowned Vermont-based Bill Knowles, who has also worked with Tiger Woods and several of Wilkinson's England team-mates. Knowles, a knee reconstruction specialist and physiotherapist based at the Vermont Orthopaedic Clinic in New England, has also worked with skiers and is known for his huge personal energy as well as expertise. Mancini believes that two weeks away from the intensity of City may also help Balotelli to focus on recovery and sees potential for his prodigy to benefit from the seclusion in the same way that Wayne Rooney did at Nike World in Portland, Oregon, at the height of his personal difficulties last November.'

'He can work quietly without a problem; without the pressure that he has here,' Mancini said. 'He's gone out there to work and to improve his knee. He can work without any problems.

'When he came to us he had a problem so he's never been

100 per cent while he's been here. But he's improved with games. For him it's important to start to play regularly – then he can show the supporters he's a good player.'

Mancini admitted he would like to have his fellow Italian back in the City side for the Manchester derby on February 12, but that it was 'more important that when he comes back he can play in all the games for the rest of the season. That's more important than the derby or the week before, or the week after.'

He would not make that key date in City's calendar – his comeback match would be three days later in a Europa Cup tie in Greece. But even before he left for treatment in the States, Mario was embroiled in one further controversy – this time surrounding Wayne Rooney!

He had commented that Rooney 'was not the best striker in Manchester' – the implication being, of course, that he, Mario, was. The comment had apparently not gone down too well at Old Trafford and I am told that Rooney had grimaced when he learned of it.

But Mancini was there once again to pick up the pieces for his errant boy. Roberto said, 'I know he likes to joke sometimes. Mario has fantastic talent. He has everything he needs to be one of the best strikers but he needs to improve and work and show all these things. But it's a free world, if he wants to speak then he can speak.

'If somebody wants to say something then it is better that he says it. This is not the SAS. It's not like the war when we couldn't speak. If you want to say everything then you can say it. But it is important that he shows here his talent. For his future it's important that he improves. At the moment, this is the best league in Europe. This time is very important for him.

'I don't think he means this [about Rooney]. He is a fantastic player. United, City, United, City... [the rivalry is] normal.'

Mario came on as a 77th-minute sub for Shaun Wright-Phillips against Salonika in Greece but was unable to break the deadlock – as Dzeko and Tevez had also failed to do – in his 13-minute cameo appearance. He also appeared in the 5-0 drubbing of Notts County in the FA Cup and the 3-0 return leg of the last 32 Europa League clash with Salonika. The *Telegraph*'s Rory Smith wryly noted that the clash was a David v Goliath encounter, 'Deploying an attacking arsenal worth £95 million to overcome opponents lying ninth in the ambitiously-titled Greek Super League in a competition derided as an afterthought could be dismissed as using a cannon to kill a fly. Indeed, so valuable was Manchester City's first XI last night that it might have seemed an act of vanity. Far from it. This was a show of strength.

'For the first time, Roberto Mancini started a match with Carlos Tevez, Edin Dzeko, David Silva and Mario Balotelli - respectively purchased for £32 million, £27 million, £24 million and £22.5 million - alongside each other. Against meagre opposition, the result was a formality. Two Dzeko goals in the first 12 minutes killed the game; Yaya Toure added gloss late on.'

Twelve days after his return from injury, Mario was back on the scoresheet for City, earning his club a point in the disappointing 1-1 home draw with Fulham. Balotelli scored in the first half with a fine strike, only for Damien Duff to equalise, meaning that the Blues were now 10 points off the top of the table with just over two months of the league campaign remaining.

There had been much made of the fact that Fulham boss Mark Hughes was returning to City for the first time since his sacking led to the arrival of Mancini. Hughes did indeed seem keen to live up to his nickname, Sparky, as he flew off the handle at the end of the game – as the *Sun*'s Neil Custis explained, 'Hughes shook the hand of City boss Roberto Mancini...Mancini did not look at him, so Hughes ripped his hand from the Italian's grasp and there was very nearly a major scene. Hughes went off down the tunnel, Mancini went after him shouting something the Fulham boss could not make out.

'Sparky left his staff, many of whom were also sacked by City, to celebrate a good point and a good performance.'

Afterwards Hughes was clearly unhappy – accusing Mancini of not showing graciousness and sincerity in the handshake, 'It's probably my fault again but I'm a little bit old fashioned. I always think if you offer your hand, it should be accepted regardless of the circumstances. Sometimes it's difficult.'

But Mancini claimed Hughes had done the same to him at the corresponding fixture at Craven Cottage in the previous November.

The tit-for-tat affair looked set to overshadow Mario's great goal – but we needn't have worried...he still got the headlines as Roberto proceeded to blast him for his performance (despite that goal!). Mancini said: 'I am not happy with Balotelli. He scored a great goal but I am not happy with his performance. To me, he should play better than he did today. For the strikers it is important to score but strikers should also play for the team, not only when we have the ball but when we lose it. Afterwards they can try and score. You cannot always play well but the attitude is always important.'

In many eyes, it was an unusual attack – given the fact that Mario had salvaged a point – but it summed up two things. First, Mancini is a perfectionist who will not accept less than 100 per cent commitment. And secondly it encapsulated the relationship between him and his protégé. A former striker himself in his playing days, Roberto was determined that Mario would not waste the natural God-given talent bestowed upon him. He was determined that Balotelli would learn and develop, as he continually told the Press pack, into one of the best players in the world.

That meant developing his all-round game and not slacking off. It meant learning the importance of the team and being part of that ethic. He would continue to keep on to Mario that he wasn't the finished article and that if he wanted to become the best, he would have to work much harder and take on board his criticisms and suggestions. It was a love-hate relationship – but one that Balotelli was lucky to have. Here he had a manager who believed in him and was willing to put in the graft –where many, including Mourinho, had decided the boy was simply not worth the effort.

And Mario knew he owed a debt of gratitude to Roberto as that 2010/11 season headed towards its conclusion (culminating, of course, with that wonderful FA Cup final win). He knew he had to repay that debt – and that, plus the growing affection of the City fans, was what convinced him to stay in Manchester in 2011, and not head back to Milan. Roberto's gee-up for Mario certainly seemed to work – just a few days after he had netted against Fulham, he was on target again, this time in the 3-0 FA Cup fifth round win over

Aston Villa at home. And it was another fine finish by Mario as he latched on to a pass by Yaya Toure to slot the ball home confidently and make it 2-0.

Now Mancini was much more appreciative of Balotelli's display – especially as he had operated as a lone frontman so that his manager could give other key men (Tevez and Dezeko) a much-needed rest. Mancini said, 'I took a risk to play only Mario up front. But Mario played well and scored a fantastic goal. I was very pleased with the overall performance. This game was very important for us.'

Those words of praise were much welcomed by Mario, who had gone off after 60 minutes with a slight injury. 'After the big stick, Roberto now became the loving surrogate dad with Mario once again,' I was told. 'It is how Roberto believes Mario best reacts. He is an enigmatic player who needs both love and discipline – and, luckily, Roberto knows how to handle him better than any other football manager in the world.'

Of course, then Villa boss Gerard Houllier had some-what played into City's hands by sending out an inexperienced team. Houllier's thought process was that the league was much more important – and he admitted he doubted Villa could have matched City even with their best eleven out there.

Even Villa fans conceded they were outclassed as City now set up a quarter-final with Reading. One said the 3-0 result was quite an achievement! 'All things considered, we only lost 3-0, so you could argue we are getting better and actually, there were some positives,' the Villa fan claimed. 'For most of the game we had a fairly experimental side with the likes of Delph at left back, Herd at right back, the Fonz on the right wing and Bannan in the middle. Add to that we had Gabby on the left wing, Clark in the middle and Michael Bradley starting in midfield and the result was better than the team that played here back in December and lost 4-0, so be unhappy with the result, just like me, but we should take it in our stride.'

I cannot ever see Mancini or Balotelli subscribing to that point of view for City. Both men are fiercely proud and determined that they will be winners: neither would accept second best (or worse). Mario seemed to be settling down now but, just as you thought you could predict his next move, he would go and surprise you yet again. This time it wasn't a surprise for the good: no, on Thursday 17 March, he would be sent off again. For the second time in his short career at City.

The Blues were already up against it when Dinamo Kiev came to town, having lost 2-0 in the Ukraine a week earlier in the first leg of their Europa League last 32 tie. The *Mail*'s Chris Wheeler summed up how Mario let his team-mates down, 'Everything about Mario Balotelli seems to be rash at the moment. After the bizarre allergic reaction to the grass in Kiev last week that saw Manchester City's volatile striker depart with a skin irritation and swollen face, came the quite idiotic challenge at Eastlands last night that arguably cost his team a place in the quarter-finals of the Europa League.'

Mario earned his red card for a terrible challenge on Goran Popov in the 36th minute. It meant his team-mates had to battle for Europa Cup survival for the best part of an hour with just 10 men. Mario had clearly let them – and the fans – down and was angry with himself as he left the ground later, with City exiting the competition 2-1 on aggregate despite their 1-0 win on the night.

Afterwards Mancini was clearly angry with Mario, as shown when one reporter at the post-match Press conference asked if that could be the case! 'What do you think?' Roberto grimaced. 'I'm disappointed because this was a difficult game and you can't have a stupid red card like this. It's a problem for him because Mario can be a fantastic player, but when he does stupid things like tonight it's difficult for me, for him and for the team. 'Even with 10 players we deserved to score another goal. With 11, we would have scored two or three goals and got to the quarter-finals.'

Mario admitted he felt ashamed at his lunge on the Kiev player and was upset that he had let down his team-mates. Balotelli said: 'It was not my intention to hurt anyone, I want to express my sincere apologies to Popov. I was trying my best for the team as I always do. I never tried to make contact with Popov and I certainly didn't want to hurt him.

'The tackle was poor and I'm very sorry to my team-mates that I got sent off so early in such an important game. It was not a good way to repay the manager who has shown so much faith in me or the owners and fans who have made me so welcome since I arrived from Italy.'

But his team-mates were quick to forgive him. They knew he was young and temperamental but, like Mancini, believed he would eventually be a world-beater for them. Dutch star Nigel De Jong summed up the feeling inside the City dressing room, saying, 'He is a young boy of 20 and he has to learn from his mistakes. I told him. Everyone told him. He is still part of the squad and has a lot of potential. He is a very good player but has to realise, on a professional level, you sometimes have to change your mentality.

'We are there to help him, not to criticise him or blast him away. He is still a young lad and has to learn. But he has experienced guys around him and has to listen to them. After the game he was angry and he was disappointed. Sometimes you make mistakes and Mario made his mistake. But he will get everything straight again.'

After the game, Mario was pictured getting out of his car and exchanging words with some Kiev fans, who had spotted him and been shouting abuse at him and gesticulating with their hands and fingers. 'He was driving home after the match and was already in a bad mood because he was sent off,' I was told by a City source. 'Then he got caught up in a bit of a traffic jam and the Kiev fans started having a go at him. He thought they might be chanting racist slogans at him, and got out of his car on impulse.

'But then he realised it was just a bit of banter, not racist, as a couple of the fans came over smiling and offered their hands for handshakes. It was all blown up out of proportion in the papers – there was no confrontation. Mario simply got back in his car and drove off.'

Mancini reacted to Mario's sending off by dropping him to the bench for the next match, the 2-0 Premier League loss to Chelsea. Balotelli would now go on to appear in a further seven games for the Blues as the season reached his climax, including the 1-0 FA Cup home win over Manchester United on April 16.

The campaign seemed to be fizzling out for the Italian. In those seven games he would fail to hit the back of the net and, if you looked at it on paper, his only contributions of record would be to receive another couple of yellow cards. But he would, of course, also receive the Man of the Match award for his part in the 1-0 FA Cup final win over Stoke. More of that and his other exploits in that season's FA Cup campaign in the next two chapters.

CHAPTER NINE

BANNER HEADLINES

It is no coincidence that Balotelli's arrival – and one of his best games thus far in a City shirt – would lead to the club ending 35 years of hurt. Yes, 35 years since Man City last won a major trophy. Blues fans were sick to the back teeth of the gloating of their neighbours at United – gloating that had led to the emergence of a banner a few years earlier in the Stretford End proclaiming how many years it had been since City had won a big trophy.

But when the Blues won the FA Cup in 2011 – a victory that saw Mario Balotelli declared the official Man of the Match – the gloating and the hurt finally came to an end. The waiting was over: City were back in the big-time – and that was now official.

So official that United took down that gloating banner...

When Roberto Mancini had taken over as manager in

2009, he had been well aware of the banner. Indeed, he had pledged to City fans just a few weeks after becoming boss that he 'would take that banner down' for them. That he would restore pride...and that is just what he did, with the help of his co-Italian Balotelli and a few of their friends. And Edin Dzeko had also promised that he would do his best to get rid of the banner when he spoke just before the big game against Stoke. The Bosnian striker said, 'I have heard about the banner. We want to change history and win something after a long time. I hope we will.'

The BBC reported the end of the banner in this way, 'Manchester United fans have removed the banner at Old Trafford that showed the number of years since rivals Manchester City last won a trophy. Manchester City secured their first trophy since 1976 on Saturday when they defeated Stoke in the FA Cup final. Some Reds fans wanted the banner to mark the last time City won the league.

'Manchester City's players celebrated the FA Cup triumph at Wembley at the weekend by walking around the pitch on their lap of honour with a banner of their own that read "00 Years". The mocking banner at the Stretford End of Old Trafford was a long-running wind-up by the United fans, who have just celebrated their fourth league title in five years.'

While the *Telegraph* reported, 'The "ticker" had reached 35 prior to Manchester City's 1-0 FA Cup final win over Stoke at Wembley but there had been some confusion about whether it would remain, even after Roberto Mancini's side's weekend triumph. It had been suggested it would be wound on to 43 to mark the last time City won the league title, or even stay at 35 as the Eastlands outfit had "bought" their trophy. That always seemed a far-fetched notion and there are plenty at Old Trafford who felt the banner should simply be "retired".'

Of course, the fans from both sides had their say on the end of the banner. United fans, generally, continued to try to goad their City counterparts by arguing that, surely now City had won something big, they should be celebrating that rather than 'going on' about the removal of the banner. One United fan, Dave, summed up that argument 'As a United fan I like the banner and wonder why, having had some success and won the FA Cup, City fans are so delighted with the removal of the banner rather than the winning of the trophy. If they are to repeat their success within the next 35 years, I don't think anyone would take exception to it being the Championship.'

But City fan Vian countered strongly, making the point that the banner was a pain because United fans continued to refer to it when they were winning trophies. That it was actually United fans who were more interested in winding up their neighbours than celebrating their team's success! Vian said, 'Because, Dave – the banner hurt. It was a reminder of City's conspicuous lack of success, especially during a period of United winning everything in sight. Honest City fans will tell you they hated the banner because it was absolutely spot on. So getting it pulled down is in itself an objective. That's why I didn't object to it – I thought it (through gritted teeth) fair comment.'

And lifelong City fan Claude made the point that it was now time for United fans – and other Premier League fans – to lay off Mancini, his team and the club owners. That, OK, they had spent money to turn City around, but the Cup win proved they were spending it well. Claude said, 'Funny how less than a year ago all I was told from non-City fans and the Press was that money can't buy you success. I was told repeatedly that money can buy you players, but it takes a quality manager to get them working together and apparently Mancini wasn't capable of this. Well, I think it's time to give credit where it's due and stop slagging City off!

'On a second point regarding United never buying a trophy. Over the past few years United have out-spent a lot of teams. Yes, this may have been due to their success but I think that they were just at the right place at the right time, as the Sky TV money came into football. Many teams have had winning periods over the years, but United were just lucky enough to be theirs at this time. I have supported City all my life even without winning anything – and am just glad [we are now starting] to win things.'

So just how did Balotelli, Mancini and Co bring about the end of the hurt? And the end of THAT banner at Old Trafford...the one that had also caused City fans so much pain over the years? The formula behind the winning of the FA Cup in 2011 – and the end of that 35-year heartache – was simple. Hard work, great play...and that inevitable bit of luck you need to win any major professional football tournament. It was also the culmination of 18 months of graft and wheeler dealing in the transfer marker by Mancini in turning the club into an outfit that could make the top four – and stay there.

City entered the FA Cup at the Third Round stage in January 2011 – and even then it appeared as if the Gods were shining on them. They drew Leicester City away and that in itself seemed symbolic of good fortune. Neil Young, who was terminally ill at the time, had scored City's winning goal when the Blues took on Leicester in the 1969 FA Cup Final at the old Wembley.

After a fans' campaign, the club agreed to dedicate the match to Neil – and the Blues also played their part in helping him and his family. Manchester City FC announced, 'In response to the wishes of our fans, Manchester City are dedicating the FA Cup visit to Leicester City to all-time great and Hall of Fame member Neil Young. It was Young's trusty left foot that fired the Blues to glory in the Wembley final against the Foxes in the 1969 final. That was just one of 107 goals that Young bagged in a glittering Blues career that encompassed more than a dozen years and 412 games in all competitions.

'Sadly, Neil has been ill for some time and was recently diagnosed with terminal cancer. Our supporters want to pay tribute to a true club legend, so in Neil's honour we are producing red and black scarves for the trip to Sven-Goran Eriksson's Leicester City on January 9. All fans who have bought a ticket to the game have received a voucher that entitles the bearer to a red and black scarf when a donation is made to support the family of Neil Young and the Cecilia Centre, Wythenshawe Hospital.' It was a classy, fitting tribute to a man who had brought so much happiness to City fans with that goal in '69.

And the team then did their part by dispensing with the Foxes – although it would take a replay at the Etihad to see them through. In the first match it finished all equal at 2-2 but the Blues won the replay 4-2 at home. They would need another replay in the Fourth Round after being held 1-1 at League One Notts County.

Another fine showing at the Etihad saw City through safely to Round Five – as they crushed their visitors from Nottingham 5-0. Balotelli played his part in the big win but did not manage to get on the scoresheet. It was February 21, and Mario was starting his first game of the year after being sidelined with a knee injury. He was replaced by Tevez just after the hour after suffering an accidental clash of heads – and did not appear at all happy that he was subbed.

Before the game, the *Sun* had trumpeted his return – and explained how Mancini was desperate for him to play after an unhappy spell for Dzeko, 'Mario Balotelli could be unleashed on FA Cup minnows Notts County on Sunday after battling back from injury.

'The Italian striker, 21, played 15 minutes in Tuesday's 0-0 draw at Aris [in the Europa League last-32 tie] in a first taste of action since December. City hope Super Mario's recent trip to the United States for rehab has sorted out the knee problems which have plagued him since his £22million switch from Inter Milan in August. City coach David Platt said: "Mario's done ever so well and that is why he was on the bench. By the time the weekend comes he will have another week of training under his belt. He'll be available for selection." Boss Roberto Mancini is keen to have Balotelli back after criticising the display of £27m new-boy Edin Dzeko.'

In the fifth round, Balotelli and City were drawn at home for the first time in that season's FA Cup – against Aston Villa.

Villa manager Gerard Houllier rested several senior players, saying he believed Premier League results were more

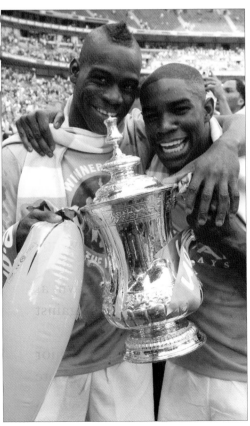

Scenes from City's 2011 FA Cup victory over Stoke City – the club's first trophy since 1976.

Away days: Balotelli in Champions League action for City against Napoli (*above* and *below left*) and in a 2011 friendly against Vancouver Whitecaps, which City won 1-0.

Above: Balotelli celebrates scoring against Napoli in 2011.

Below left: Appearing at the Naples Prosecutor's Office as a witness in an investigation into money-laundering in his home town in 2011.

Below right: Suited and booted ahead of Italy's Euro 2012 campaign.

Euro 2012: Balotelli lines up for Italy during their campaign.

Above: Balotelli makes an attempt on goal during Italy's Euro 2012 match against England.

Below: Giving a thumbs-up to the crowd after Italy beat England on penalties to go through to the semi-finals.

Above and below left: Balotelli in action for Italy in the Euro 2012 final against Spain.

Below right: Balotelli is inconsolable after Spain beat Italy to become European champions.

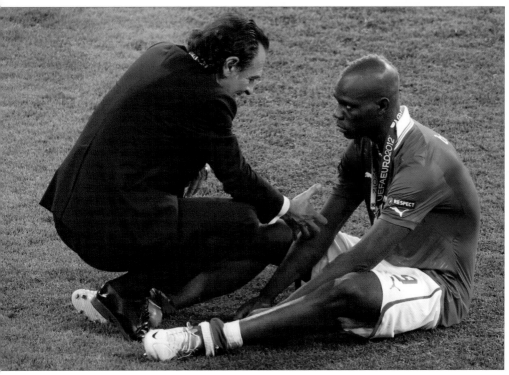

Above: Balotelli is congratulated by Spanish players as he goes to collect his Euro 2012 runner-up medal.

Below: Italian coach Cesare Prandelli comforts Balotelli after the Euro 2012 final.

Above: Balotelli meets Italian president Giorgio Napoletano after Italy's Euro 2012 campaign.

Below: One of the most famous – and infamous – footballers in the world, Balotelli is mobbed by fans wherever he goes.

important. But Mancini – who now was increasingly started to believe City could win the FA Cup – fielded a strong line-up. The boss's decision paid dividends as the Blues ran out comfortable 3-0 winners at the Etihad. And Balotelli weighed in with his first FA Cup goal for the club. His goal was sandwiched in between Yaya Toure's opener and David Silva's effort.

The *Sun* led the way in praising Balotelli for his show – but also pointing out that the dark side to the boy always loomed beneath the surface, 'Roberto Mancini demanded Mario Balotelli stepped up to the plate. Last night, he did so in spectacular fashion to leave Manchester City a match away from Wembley. Mancini had questioned the striker's work rate ahead of the FA Cup tie and told him he needed to do more.

'And this was more like it as the wonderfully-talented 20-year-old lead the line, with the skill in evidence for City's second goal in no doubt. His half volley from Yaya Toure's superb through ball was a thing of beauty and his 10th goal of the season. City boss Mancini said: "He played well and it was a wonderful goal."

'But as ever with Balotelli, controversy and confusion always seem to follow him around. The confusion was on the face of Toure, who was asked by Balotelli in the first half to give up his gloves because he was feeling a bit chilly. The controversy was on 58 minutes when he lead with his elbow and caught Chris Herd in the face as they jostled for a high ball.

'It was a challenge that enraged the Villa players and some on the bench.

'Luckily for the Italian, Mark Clattenburg was refereeing

and he does not seem to think such offences are a problem. Although unlike Wayne Rooney's elbow at Wigan on Saturday, the ref did at least show a yellow card. Two minutes after that incident Balotelli was hauled off by Mancini to save him from Villa retribution. But despite all the hullabaloo that ended his contribution, he had fully played his part in a dominant City performance in this fifth-round clash.'

And the *Telegraph*'s Mark Ogden also paid tribute to Balotelli's talent, saying the boy had 'the grace of a panther', '...City had one foot in the quarter-finals by half-time following Balotelli's strike on 25 minutes. The enigmatic Italian forward has endured an injury-hit campaign at Eastlands, but he possesses a prodigious ability to find the back of the net and his finish from Toure's clipped pass emphasised his talent.

'With the grace of a panther, Balotelli escaped three Villa defenders before beating Brad Friedel with a first-time shot from 20 yards. Balotelli, sporting a white stripe haircut which suggested he was auditioning for a role in Gremlins, has now scored 10 goals in 16 games for City – and collected nine bookings – yet Mancini continues to call for more from the 20-year-old.

'The disciplinary demons that have also tormented Balotelli this season resurfaced, however, when he was booked by referee Mark Clattenburg after catching full-back Chris Herd in the face with his arm on 57 minutes. Having missed Wayne Rooney's elbow on James McCarthy at Wigan on Saturday, Clattenburg was clearly in zero-tolerance mode for this game, but while Balotelli's flailing arm was clumsy, it was more PG than X-rated in comparison to the Rooney incident.'

The excellent City website, bluedays.co.uk, commented on how Balotelli could be brilliant at times – and how his goal was one of the best of the season, 'After the morale sapping draw against Fulham it was just the start City needed. With a side set up to be patient, City could then do just that. Villa didn't change their game plan and continued to sit deep, hoping to catch us on the counter. Mancini wasn't falling for that, and as a result we spent much of the time knocking the ball around in our own half.

'Overall it wasn't a great spectacle, though that was forgotten when Villa pushed sufficiently forward for Yaya to hit a beautifully weighted pass over the top. Balotelli timed his run across and behind the Villa defence so finely that he was able to ease up as he approached the ball. The subsequent half-volley was as good a strike as we've seen all season.

'That's the second great finish in as many games from the Italian 20-year-old, and we're now starting to see why he has the "Super Mario" moniker. The rest of his game still left plenty of room for improvement, but the biggest concern was another spell of limping after a knock on his knee.'

Meanwhile, Mancini declared himself delighted with Balotelli's contribution – especially, as he conceded, it could have been a tough night for the striker playing up front alone, 'I took a risk to play only Mario up front. But Mario played well and scored a fantastic goal. I was very pleased with the overall performance. This game was very important for us.'

Indeed it was – and a home draw in the sixth round would also help keep spirits high. City were duly drawn out of the hat with Reading at the Etihad and would now power to the semis at Wembley with another strong performance – this time against the only non-Premier League outfit still in the competition. Reading proved solid and stubborn but the Blues eventually broke them down thanks to a late winner from Micah Richards. The Blues had needed little motivation to beat the Royals – as the winners would play in the semi-finals...against Manchester United.

Balotelli had not been included in the starting line-up after suffering an allergic reaction in the previous match at Dinamo Kiev that had led to him being sick on the pitch. He appeared as a sub for Patrick Vieira on 70 minutes – and four minutes later Richards was in the right place at the right time to send City to Wembley and that showdown with neighbours United.

The *Telegraph*'s Henry Winter brilliantly summed up what the win – and the clash with United – now meant to City and their wonderful army of loyal fans, 'Blue Moon rising, Red Devils waiting. Manchester City have booked themselves an FA Cup semi-final with Manchester United with this occasionally edgy victory over Reading. Micah Richards's header eventually pointed them to Wembley, triggering huge celebrations here.

'The outpouring of emotion at the final whistle reflected how long City have been waiting. They have not been in an FA Cup semi-final since 1981. They have not met United in the last four since the General Strike was on, Agatha Christie was vanishing and John Logie Baird was demonstrating the flickering wizardry of his magic box.

'That 1926 semi saw City prevail 3-0 over United at Bramall Lane before losing the final to Bolton Wanderers, who have been drawn against Stoke City in the other semi.

The weight of history hangs heavily on City. Their search for a first trophy since 1976 is mocked by United fans, such serial winners under Sir Alex Ferguson. "Thirty-six years but we're still here," chanted the City fans defiantly on Sunday. No wonder they erupted in celebration when Lee Probert drew this game to a close. They chanted Roberto Mancini's name. They threw around plastic blue dolphins, a paddling pool, inflatable bananas and countless beach-balls. They did the Poznan celebration, jumping up and down with their backs to the pitch, arms draped across each other's shoulders like they were auditioning for the Folies Bergère.'

City's official website also stressed how significant the win was, 'City's expectant fans had to wait 75 minutes before they could go bananas, and it was their long-time favourite Micah Richards who unlocked Reading's defence where City's front line had faltered. For all the Blues' expensive firepower mounted against their Championship challengers, it was a towering header from Richards at a David Silva corner that finally booked a Wembley showdown with Manchester United. Richards, who also joined in that Notts goalfest a month earlier, was waiting to make his mark and keep City on the glory trail. The dream of an FA Cup victory, in the year of 1969 hero Neil Young's passing, lives on.'

Now the build-up would begin in earnest for that semi-final against United as City aimed to make it an FA Cup semi-final record of nine victories out of 11 as they strove to reach the FA Cup Final for the first time since 1981. The *Sun*'s Neil Custis set the scene for the clash at the home of English football, saying, 'There are derbies and there are derbies. Then there is Manchester City versus Manchester United at Wembley for a place in the FA Cup final. Ooooh goodness this is a big one. Since City became the richest club in world football an already fierce rivalry has been cranked up. The "noisy neighbours" as Alex Ferguson labels those in the blue half have got under his skin. But invariably it has been Fergie coming out on top with late goals. The unforgettable 4-3 at Old Trafford last season, Paul Scholes' late winner here. Then there was the most intense of Carling Cup semis, when City won the first leg 2-1, United came back to claim a place in the final with a 3-1 in the return. Only last month at Old Trafford Rooney scored one of the greatest derby goals with his overhead kick.

'The last time these two rivals met in an FA Cup semi-final was 1926 when City won 3-0 only to then lose to, guess who, Bolton, who are in this season's other semi. The last time City were at Wembley was 12 years ago. Then it was for a League One play-off final which they won in quite dramatic circumstances. This is for a place in an FA Cup final in the first-ever meeting between the two at the home of English football. City have not been in an FA Cup semi-final or final for 30 years. In 1981 they lost to Tottenham in a replay famous for Ricky Villa's incredible winner. They have not put their hands on any silverware for 35 years – and United will be keen to keep it that way.'

Yes, it was a tie that had everything – and one that City, and Balotelli as he searched for his first silverware in the English game, were desperate to win. One match at Wembley that would leave them one match from a return to Wembley, in the final of the FA Cup.

On a great day for the blue side of Manchester, City would beat United 1-0 with a winning goal from Yaya Toure as Balotelli played his part with a stirring performance – and a celebration that would, typically, also hog the headlines! City proved superior on the day, and deserved their win, as the Press corps made clear. ITV also made the point that not only had City earned themselves a day of potential glory in the final – they had also ended United's dreams of another treble, 'Manchester City ended Manchester United's treble bid by booking their first FA Cup final appearance since 1981 in a game that saw Paul Scholes sent off. Man of the match Yaya Toure was City's second-half matchwinner, seizing on a catastrophic blunder by Michael Carrick before finishing smartly past Edwin van der Sar for the only goal of the game...It means there will be no repeat of 1999 for United, who must concentrate on their bid for glory in the Premier League and Champions League. City, watched by chairman Khaldoon al-Mubarak, have the chance to "change history" as Mancini has demanded, and will return to Wembley on May 14 to face either Bolton or Stoke looking to collect their first trophy in 35 years.

'Unfortunately, firebrand Mario Balotelli threatened to put a dampener on celebrations when he unwisely rejoiced in front of the United fans, triggering a shoving match with Anderson and an angry reaction from Rio Ferdinand – who also squared up to City coach David Platt.'

Afterwards Mancini said, 'I am very happy for our supporters, because they deserve this. It is important to start winning trophies, and I stand by my claim that if we win the FA Cup this year we can try for the title next season. This could be a turning point for us, but it is important to remember there is another game to win. I think we can go on from this to win the FA Cup and secure a top-four finish.'

In stark contrast, Sir Alex Ferguson would not talk to the papers...City and their win had clearly got under his skin.

The *Guardian* was able to shed more light on the Balotelli incident, 'Some United players were incensed after Mario Balotelli approached rival supporters while tugging at the City badge on his shirt; his team-mates had gathered towards the other end of the pitch. Anderson and Rio Ferdinand reacted furiously and attempted to shove the Italian striker away from the sidelines, prompting the City coach, David Platt, and manager, Roberto Mancini, to intervene. Ferdinand was further angered when Balotelli winked at him; the United defender then confronted Platt, asking him to "control his players".'

Ferdinand would later use his Twitter account to comment on his and Mario's actions, 'If you score a goal and give a bit to opposing fans I kind of accept that, but at the final whistle go to your own fans and enjoy it, not opposing fans. If I offended anyone I apologise. Emotions were obviously running high.'

United winger Nani added about Balotelli, 'He was showing his badge to our fans. Anderson just took him out from in front of our fans. Rio was very angry because it is not fair, it was very disrespectful to do that in front of the fans. We were not happy with that.'

But it wasn't as bad as United were trying to make out – certainly the FA agreed with that analysis, refusing to take any action against Balotelli, or indeed Ferdinand.

Certainly the City fans themselves were delighted that the Italian had showed his allegiance to the shirt in front of United's demoralised supporters. It elevated him even higher in their affections – here was a player after their own heart!

'He showed he cared for the club by doing what he did,' Eddie, one lifelong City fan told me. 'It took some guts to go up to the United end and do that – or maybe was just that Mario IS actually as mad as people make out! Whatever, he consolidated his position as one of the City terrace idols by sticking one up at our bitterest rivals!'

City midfielder Patrick Vieira was quick to defend Balotelli, with whom he had played at Inter Milan. He said Mario was not being deliberately provocative or out to cause trouble, but that he was just thrilled with the win and wanted everyone to know, 'That's part of his personality, that's Balotelli's charm,' the Frenchman said. 'I don't think it was a case of provocation, I just think he got carried away. There was more pressure on City's shoulders than United's. As a club and as a team, United are more used to controlling these types of games. For us, it was pure joy because the club has been waiting for this for so long. And with all the press expecting United to win easily, it was a big relief. There was some over-excitement, but I think United's players got carried away as well.'

Months later Mario would finally open up about the bust-up with Ferdinand, saying, 'I didn't ever speak to him. But I don't have anything against him. I just showed him the shirt of City. Obviously he got angry with me. But for me what happened on the pitch stayed on the pitch and now we are friends like before. Or we respect each other anyway. I'm going to give him the handshake before the game like I give to everyone. He's a great player.'

After the match at Wembley, Nani would reveal how much the defeat to City had stunned United – and tried to play down the impact it could have on their season, 'We are very disappointed but we are experienced enough to forget this game and think about the games coming up. The other trophies we are competing for are more important than this one. If we'd had to sacrifice one trophy from the three this would have been the one.

'We would prefer to win the Champions League and the Premier League. But we must still recover quickly because we have Newcastle on Tuesday and have lots of games coming up after that. We must be ready for them. It's very important we win the next game.'

Pablo Zabaleta was, naturally enough, upset and angry by Scholes' high challenge on him with 20 minutes to go. The Argentine certainly felt it warranted a sending-off and said it could have been a lot worse given the England midfielder attacked him with his studs up. 'It was as really bad tackle, very high, over the knee,' said Zabaleta. 'If it had been any lower my knee would probably be gone. I have pain in my quad, but it was a really bad challenge.'

From Mario and City's point of view the defeat of United also meant that they had upset the Red Devils' dream of 'doing another Treble' – even though eventually Barcelona would also kill off that fantasy in the Champions League final.

Midfield hardman Nigel de Jong said the win had been achieved because the City players were so determined to achieve it – to the extent that they had a 'clear-the-air' debate at half-time. The Dutchman said, 'We all want to win and sometimes you come face to face with each other. It happened in the dressing room and it is just a small thing. But it keeps the fire alive. Everyone wants to win the main prizes and we showed a great spirit in the second half. The belief has always been there. Obviously we've had our ups and downs and that's normal for a team that wants to progress. But in the second half we showed that belief. We came out of the dressing room and dominated United.

'We also put a statement for the club. It's a big step forwards for us. Everyone has been talking about City spending all this money and seeking out prizes, and now we're only one game away from winning our first silverware. For me, the guys are hungry but you've got to start somewhere in feeding that hunger. We did that against United.

'Now we must make a final push to take this club forward and make it happen. United have so many prizes but City is a big club as well. And now you have two clubs in Manchester dominating two of the competitions. History is a big part of this club but we are trying to change that history. But we just have to maintain our focus now. Our main goal this season was a top-four finish. This result will give us a big boost in confidence for the last six games of the season. We have to take a Champions League place because, otherwise, winning the FA Cup would all be for nothing. We can't just have one. We have to go for both. We can enjoy having reached the FA Cup final, but we have to focus on finishing in the top four too because we have important games to play.'

And fellow midfielder Gareth Barry was also quick to point out that the pressure was now on – but that is just what the team wanted. To win the FA Cup – and end that 35 years of hurt - Roberto Mancini's side would have to beat a real dogs-of-war team in Stoke City at Wembley.

Barry predicted that winning one trophy would lead to

many more. He said: 'The final is going to be as tough or even tougher than beating United in the semi. The pressure will be more on us, so we've got to learn from the United game and take that into the final. It is a massive moment for the club to reach the final. It has been a long wait. So it is important now that we win it. The next game is going to be just as tough, with the pressure maybe more on us.

'It is about winning that first trophy. It was mentioned at the beginning of the season.

'If we can win that trophy, then maybe more will follow. The first one is always the most difficult one. There were a few great individual performances against United but it was the perfect team performance. We all stuck together, as you have to do to beat Manchester United. Hopefully that will show we are together as a group.'

At the time, Barry was under pressure from everyone's least favourite villain, Joey Barton. The QPR player had claimed that Barry was only in the City and England teams because he was a 'teacher's pet'. But Barry, wisely, said he preferred to do his talking on the pitch, 'You approach every game trying to do your best. I always do. If you get criticism, you get criticism. That's the game. You try and respond to it. I always give 100 per cent. If it's good enough, you get selected again. If it's not...I don't really want to speak about another professional, positive or negative.'

Belgian defender Vincent Kompany, who captained City to their victory over United at Wembley, was convinced that the win would now give the Blues the belief to compete regularly for top honours. He told *The Times*, 'I believe when you win games like this it should give you belief for the rest of the season. There is no question about us competing. We are among the top five teams at the moment who are competing for a Champions League spot. I think we are respected but everything takes time. It's logical that a team that has been winning so many years gets the benefit of having that extra respect, but we are learning and if we can win this FA Cup, which is not going to be easy at all, it will be the first step towards what we are trying to do.'

The 25-year-old also said he believed City were closing the gap on United, 'There is still a gap between us and the team who are going to be champions but that gap is not in the games we play against each other. The difference is in how we compete with other teams. It's been close in many derby games before this and it was going to happen for us sooner or later.'

Meanwhile, goal hero Yaya Toure wanted to pay tribute to his brother Kolo, who at the time was facing a suspension. Kolo would eventually be handed a six-month ban from all football for failing a drugs test.

And Yaya said after the win over United, 'I am very sad for him at this moment in time. He is a professional player and he wants to play. People make mistakes sometimes. It is part of life. It is part of sport. Mentally, he is a strong guy. He is the most important person in my life. Every time I speak with him he helps me. I dedicate this win to him and the fans.'

Yaya also told how he was delighted for the fans who had supported him since his arrival from Barcelona. He said, 'I am very happy. We have beaten our big rivals, which is fantastic and we are going to enjoy it. I am really happy for the fans. They have been waiting 35 years for a trophy. It is a long time. I think this is going to be the year for

Manchester City. But it is not finished. We have to take a second step – we have to reach the Champions League and we are working towards that.'

City assistant boss Brian Kidd said that he felt the club were well on the road to achieving that second step – and beyond – because of the team spirit in the camp, which was similar to what he had experienced when he was assistant to Alex Ferguson at Man United in the 90s. 'Manchester United won the FA Cup in 1990, then the Cup Winners' Cup the following season,' Kidd told Sky Sports. 'They lost the league to Leeds the following year, which proved to be the prelude to what they are now. Recovering from that setback showed how much spirit there was at Old Trafford. I feel there is a lot of that with City.'

He also said he felt City's surge was great for the city itself, 'It is great for Manchester football. I was looking round just before kick-off. I saw one half of the stadium red, the other blue. For me personally, it was a wonderful moment. You can have wonderful nights playing against the best teams in Europe. That is what we are striving for.

'But we can only enjoy this win for a couple of hours, then we must prove our mettle. After 35 years, now we have a chance to win a trophy. It is all a learning process for our players but when you do win something, it is intoxicating. You should just become hungrier for even more.'

The last words after the win over United that would lay the foundations for glory at the Etihad lay with the boss, Mancini, and rightly so given that he had masterminded the marvellous triumph. Speaking in his post-match press conference, Mancini joked when asked about Balotelli and whether he should be punished. He said, 'Every time it's

Balotelli's fault but I want to wait. I didn't see what happened so it's difficult to say. We can put him in jail? Next week we can put him in jail for this.'

He then turned to serious mode by affirming that he believed City had deserved their win. He said, 'United played very well in the first 25 minutes. They had good chances to score. After that we deserved to win the game. It's difficult to play against Manchester United. They are some team, not an easy team. They are used to playing this game every year. For us, it's the first time after a long time.

'Today we have only won the semi-final. I'm very happy for the supporters. They have never had a day like this afternoon but for us it's important we forget. We still have to play another game. Probably the final will be harder than this. Today, for me, was important. I would like to win this cup for the club, the supporters and all the people who work at Manchester City. We beat United in an important game but I don't want, "Ah, we beat United but it's finished".

'I believe that for us it's important to start to win the first trophies. If we win the FA Cup, next year we can win the [league] title.'

It was a bold, brave prediction – but these were bold, brave times at Manchester City. With the iron-discipline of Mancini and the flamboyance of his countryman Balotelli they now approached the future confidently. But first up was that all-important FA Cup final – and the chance to finally put to bed the haunting spectre of those 35 years without a major trophy.

CHAPTER TEN

END OF
THE HURT

Those 35 years of hurt for Manchester City and their fans finally came to a welcome end on 11 May, 2011. That was the day when they banished the misery of all those years without winning a major trophy. It was also the day when Mario Balotelli proved conclusively that he DID have the talent on the football field to back up his larger-than-life antics off it – as he was named the Man of the Match after a fine performance at Wembley as City beat Stoke City 1-0 to lift the FA Cup.

The bookmakers paddypower.com set the scene well for an occasion that had City as favourites, with the battlers of Stoke rank outsiders, 'Billionaires Manchester City the firm favourites. Despite their recent lack of silverware and the fact that it's their first appearance in the FA Cup Final since a certain Ricky Villa ended their hopes in 1981,

Manchester City are the firm 8/11 favourites to win their fifth FA Cup.

'Whilst never seriously threatening to take the Premier League title this season, Roberto Mancini's side have gradually improved and look set to claim their place in next season's lucrative Champions League. A lot of money has been spent on City's attack – Carlos Tevez, Mario Balotelli and Edin Dzeko cost over £100 million between them – but it has been City's defensive solidity that has been the key to their success this season. They have only conceded three goals in this season's tournament, and none since Neal Bishop's goal for Notts County threatened an upset in the Fourth Round. Clean sheets against Aston Villa, Reading and neighbours Manchester United have carried them to their first FA Cup final in thirty years and Stoke's biggest problem will be penetrating an impressive rearguard.

'Vincent Kompany will captain City if Carlos Tevez fails to recover from the injury he sustained against Liverpool and, alongside Joleon Lescott, forms one of the best central defensive partnerships in the league. Tevez's injury is City's main concern ahead of the final, with neither Mario Balotelli nor Edin Dzeko showing anything like the form that prompted Roberto Mancini to spend the best part of £60 million.'

Well, now was the chance – and the perfect time – for Mario to show he was worth the money Mancini had invested in him. Before the Final, Mario told the Press that he was actually a sweet, shy guy and that the image of him as a brash exhibitionist was far from the reality, 'My public image is absolutely not a fair reflection of who I am. Sometimes I do the wrong thing and there are things I regret but I'm 20. People who know me are aware I'm not a bad guy but I'm shy; I stay at home and play on the PlayStation and sometimes I go shopping. In Italy, I have a lot of friends I can do things with. When I was at home on a day off, I would go to the shooting range, or do a lesson of [martial art] Muay Thai or go-karting.

'Next year it will be easier. My friends will come over and I think my family will move here. The idea people have of me is not correct. Absolutely not. I am shy. I like to have fun. People tell me some of the things that are said about me and many times I have to laugh because these things just aren't true. I like to do normal things, but maybe not normal for a footballer.'

He was asked why Mourinho had labelled him 'unmanageable'. Mario said, 'Maybe Mourinho said I was unmanageable because he could not do it. Roberto Mancini is managing me now, so what Mourinho said is not true. They are both great managers but they are different. When I had problems with Mourinho, he tried to work against me; Mancini has supported me. Mancini killed me in the dressing room after I was sent off against Kiev [in the Europa League], he told me: "You're an idiot, I don't know why I buy you and why I bother with you" but, with the press, he speaks well of me. The problem with Mourinho and me was that we are the same kind of character.'

No wonder Balotelli shuddered when it was then suggested that Mourinho might eventually end up as his boss at City if they got rid of Mancini, 'Why? City are fourth in the league, we are in the FA Cup final for the first time in 30 years. I don't know why somebody would want another coach. Roberto is doing very well; why should he be changed?

Roberto never lies. He says what he has to say; that's what I like about him. I trust Roberto.'

But he did have something to prove to the City fans who had stood by him. His record before the FA Cup final of ten goals, 11 bookings and one red card did not add up to the brilliance they were expecting after his transfer from Italy. Mario conceded that he had not done as well as he himself had even hoped, and tried to explain why, 'I can't look back on a single game at City and think, "This is how I want to play." I have a normal level and another, higher level. I think that when I play at the normal level I can be one of the best but, in England, I have never played at that level. This year was difficult because I was injured twice and I didn't train properly in pre-season. I didn't know if I was coming to City or staying with Inter, so I never trained and my condition was really low. I haven't played so good but I still think I can enjoy English football. It's more physical but it's easier than Italian football, especially for a striker.'

Then he spoke about the incident in the semi against United – when he went to celebrate in front of their fans – that had left Rio Ferdinand so angry. Balotelli said, 'I think United players were too sensitive about it. I showed my shirt but I didn't swear.

'But I'm sensitive as well. And, if one of them did the same to me, maybe I'd react the same. It's normal that, when you lose a game, you're upset and if another player celebrates like that you'll be angry. But when I lose my temper it's because I decide to. If I do something it's because I want to do it.'

Many fans – and not just of City and Stoke – felt the decision to play the FA Cup final on the same day as Premier League matches was well out of order. The FA had decreed that it should be that way as the Champions League Final was to be held at Wembley two weeks later. And the fans felt that the decision took away something of the special aura of the occasion.

One fan said, 'What is the FA cup final doing on a day when there are league fixtures? I may come over as all "when I were a lad" but the FA Cup Final always signified the end of the season and long summers that were ahead. This now typifies all that is wrong with the game - the Champions league is put first, no doubt driven by Sky's money, meaning the FA cup final essentially becomes "just another game".'

And another football fan, Elliott, added, 'I agree that the FA Cup Final should be the last domestic game of the season. Unfortunately those at the FA obviously don't agree as they've bent over backwards to get the Champions League Final at Wembley, meaning no other events are to be held at the stadium two weeks ahead of the game (as stated by UEFA). I've read they've also had some of the taxes written off for this game too, as UEFA weren't happy about how high they were. They should get their priorities right because they're becoming a laughing stock, especially after the World Cup bid.'

And Harap said, 'Agree, it is a shame about the cup final being almost overshadowed, it doesn't feel right. I'm hoping Man City win it personally, used to go see them quite a bit when I was at uni in Manchester and always had a bit of a soft spot for them.' City fans agreed that the final should have been given more precedence but it did not dampen the enthusiasm of the thousands who headed for Wembley in May, 2011, both with and without tickets.

City had the lion's share of possession and were the better

team during the 90 minutes. The website soccernews.com highlighted the fact that very fact and Balotelli's importance in the goal, saying, 'Both managers fielded their strongest line-ups as Carlos Tevez came through a late fitness test for City, as did Matthew Etherington and Robert Huth for Tony Pulis' Stoke. And it was the favourites who started the stronger.

'Tevez took just five minutes before he tested Thomas Sorensen in the Stoke goal with a low drive, with Ryan Shawcross fortunate not to score an own goal as he deflected a low Aleksander Kolarov cross into the side netting. It was all City in the opening half-hour as Toure fired a shot inches wide from 35 yards, before Sorensen produced a sensational save, somehow pushing Mario Balotelli's curling effort past the far post when it appeared the Italian had surely scored from just inside the area.

'[Then] Silva failed to even have a shot at goal when Tevez played him through on goal early in the second-half. Stoke were much improved, though, and City were indebted to Joe Hart for saving well when Kenwyne Jones had a shot from six yards out after chasing a long ball and getting the better of Joleon Lescott. It appeared certain that the game was going to go into extra-time as neither side was able to make any real impression going forward as full-time drew near. But with 16 minutes left, City made the breakthrough.

'It was a scrappy goal in truth – not that City will mind – as Silva looked to combine with Tevez down the left. When the ball was played into the box Balotelli's effort hit Marc Wilson and fell perfectly for Toure to run on and smash a left-footed effort past Sorensen from eight yards. The goal sparked scenes of wild celebration in the City end and appeared to knock the wind out of Stoke, who never looked likely to recover as Mancini's men hung on to claim the first trophy of the Sheikh Mansour era.'

Yes, the match was finally won – and so too the cup. Mario had played a key role in the goal, linking up with Silva as they finally set up Yaya for the strike that broke Stoke's heart and led to City fans finally being able to celebrate the end of the wilderness years. They had won a major trophy once again – 35 years on.

The *Telegraph*'s Jeremy Wilson best summed up Balotelli's mature display in the final, saying, 'It [The win] was as much a triumph at Wembley on Saturday for the astute man-management of Roberto Mancini as the deep pockets of Sheikh Mansour. And there was no one who underlined that fact better than Mario Balotelli, the enfant terrible of the Premier League, whose man of the match performance was followed by an interview that will live almost as long in the memory. Asked if it had been his best performance of the season, he paused briefly before offering an assessment of absolute candour. "All my season was s***," he said. "Can I say that? I've played not very well, but today maybe I played more for the team." An apology followed from ITV presenter Adrian Chiles but, after a game in which he had performed with absolute discipline, the absence of any verbal restraint was perhaps predictable...continued his torment of Stoke right back Andy Wilkinson. Both his vision and technique was evident as he dissected the Stoke defence for David Silva to deliver the pass into the penalty area that led to City's winning goal.'

After the game, Mario admitted he was delighted to have helped City team to win the FA Cup and his own role –

which ended with that Man of the Match award. 'All my season, maybe it wasn't good,' he said. 'Today maybe I played more for the team, so it was good. Every player has his quality and I have my quality. If I show my qualities for the team I can be important. It feels good to win. I said before the game that we are better than them but we have to respect them as they are a team. You have to go on the pitch with respect but you have to give everything.'

Mario also said the City fans had been 'brilliant' and thanked them for their support and constant encouragement as they searched for the killer goal. Micah Richards and Adam Johnson also chipped in with thanks to the supporters who had waited so long for this moment. 'It is the biggest cup competition in the world and we have won it,' said Johnson. 'Look what it means to the fans after 35 years of waiting for it.'

And Richards said: 'It is unbelievable. We have worked hard all season and we have won The FA Cup – I can't believe it. This is the start. This is the first [trophy] and the most important. It is exciting times for us. We will spend in the summer and be better next year.'

And keeper Joe Hart, whose brilliant save thwarted Kenwyne Jones from putting Stoke in front just before Toure scored, said it was time for City to now step out of United's shadow. Hart said, 'I couldn't care less about Man Utd. It's about what happens with us.

'We beat the best. We beat a very good Stoke team today. A bit more consistency next season and you never know.'

Yaya Toure himself would later say that the FA Cup win was the greatest moment of his career – quite a comment when you consider that he won TEN trophies with

Barcelona, including the Champions League in 2009. He explained that it was so special because he was delighted to be 'making history' at his new club – that he was a key part of the history making.

The Ivory Coast star also indicated that he believed the win was down to the spirit Mancini had brought to the club. He told the *Daily Mail*: 'I think our team bond developed during last season and we were strong at the end. We can continue this next season hopefully. Although I scored the winning goals in the semi-final and final, both of those victories were down to us being a strong team.

'Scoring those goals at Wembley was amazing – the cup final goal was the best moment of my career. I came here to make history and I did that.'

Skipper Vinny Kompany also believed that the win would open the floodgates to other trophies. The Belgian centre-back said, 'In my opinion, this is just the first of many trophies to come in the future. We've laid the first brick, now we can build a house.

'We knew Stoke would make it hard. All credit to them, they kept the fight going until the last minute, but if you look at the chances we deserved to win. This is how far we've come. If this isn't a step forward, I don't know what is.'

And Dutch midfielder Nigel de Jong added: 'The feeling is unbelievable. We've worked so hard to win this FA Cup, and this was for all our fans. The city will be blue for a long time! We deserved it because we dominated from the first minute, though they came back with their set pieces. I missed out on a World Cup medal in the summer, but I'll happily take this.'

Boss Mancini dedicated the win to the long-suffering fans,

many of whom had waited since 1976 for this wonderful moment. He had also won a Champions League spot for the club – and was, like Mario, becoming a cult hero among the fans. 'I am happy for the fans, they deserved to win this Cup. For a long time they didn't win. My feeling is good, but it's important that they also feel good.'

He added, 'I feel very good. I used to watch the FA Cup Final on TV when I was young, now we have won it. I am very proud. I'm happy. Congratulations to all my players because I think that this afternoon they played a fantastic game. We deserved to score in the first half but were really unlucky. We always had the game under control, but in football if you don't score then anything can happen at any moment. Yaya is a fantastic player but it wasn't only about Yaya. It was all the players – and those who didn't play today – who helped us win this trophy.'

City coach David Platt expanded upon that line – pointing out that Mancini had won the Italian Cup first as boss of Inter Milan, and that had led to further trophies. 'Champions League qualification was for the business end of the club, it makes the club more attractive to players that we might want to bring in and that was important, but for the dressing room we had to win something,' Platt told BBC Radio 5 live. 'You ask Roberto which of the trophies was the best while he was at Inter and he will say it was the first Italian Cup because that is what gave the dressing room that winning mentality. What nobody can take away from the players is that they have won something.

'Getting to the FA Cup final was terrific after beating Manchester United in the semi-final, but now there are a lot of people going back up the motorway very happy because having won something for the first time in 35 years, it is a major trophy.

'What's important for Robbie is that he wins for the supporters and he wins for the owners but he will put that away now and concentrate on the next one.'

The fans were deliriously happy with Mancini too – and the result – although there were already some murmurings that Tevez might not want to stay and help bring more glory to the club. One fan said, 'Congratulations to City – may you stay on a winning streak. After a 35-year wait, I hope the City of Manchester does you proud. Stay with City, Carlos, more silver is on its way. And you are one of the best.'

But another fan voiced the belief that it might be best if Carlos departed, saying, 'Tevez would be a thorn in the side of City if he stays. I appreciate what he has done for the club however he is nothing more than a drifter. The less playing time he gets the more frustrated and childish he gets. For the good of the team and the future, Tevez must be traded this summer. Mancini said he wanted to start a tradition of winning, a tradition of success, well so far Hart, Kompany, De Jong, Richards, Balo, David, Johnson, Dzeko they all seem part of that future. They are City's future. I simply just don't see Tevez there. He is not part of the future for City. I expect City to be quite lively this upcoming transfer window.'

Other supporters simply told of their exhilaration – and celebrations! – after the marvellous win. One said, 'Absolutely lost my mind today. Was bought more shots than I can even count and I was out cold. What an absolutely magical, brilliant, un****ingbelievable day.' Another said, 'The world belongs to Manchester City FC. When I got home

I was pissed, emotional drained. Apart from that goal...and the lifting of the Cup, I couldn't remember anything about the match. I can remember now, and those memories will live with me for the rest of my life. I have a hangover that I haven't had for 35 years...and I love it.'

Another City fan exclaimed, 'I can't and at the moment don't want to be objective about the final. The result and winning that trophy has finally exorcised the demons of 1981 for me. Me and my dad hugged and cried at the final whistle, while my lad was jumping around (oh to be young again!)'

Lifelong fan Roy elucidated more about the actual game – and how City dominated. He said, 'Gotta say we normally storm our opponents for 10 minutes then relax. That's the first game all season we played attacking football for 90 minutes. All the players played their hearts out so in the end Stoke didn't stand a chance. I have to ask why can't we play like that every game? If we did I think we would have been fighting for the title this year but no point crying over spilt milk. It just shows the quality and potential we have in our squad and how well they are when they want to be. What a game and what a result.'

City fanatic Kevin would later say, 'Just getting sober and back home from one of the best days of my life. We were everything we hoped we would be and completely wiped the floor with Stoke. Met thousands of fans.... had fantastic seats too. Man, yesterday was better than sex. Thank you City and well done to all the fans at Wembley...for an atmosphere only an FA cup final can make.'

Another fan of many years, Harry Clay, said he had been 'really pleased' for Balotelli and pleased that the Italian had finally got his act together. He said, 'We all knew he was a

176

boy with immense talent but we had started to wonder if he would ever live up to it. He was starting to get headlines for things other than football and I wondered if his heart was really in the game, let alone our football club. He seemed distracted by off-field events that were happening and didn't seem 100 per cent committed to City. There was the feeling among some fans that he was only surviving because of his close relationship with the manager – that if he hadn't been as close to Mancini he would have at least have been told to buckle down more and prove himself. He needed to show his team-mates that he cared about them and winning things with City – and at Wembley against Stoke he did just that.

'The Cup Final win was a turning point for Balotelli's relationship with the fans and probably some of the players too. He showed us he DID care – that he would go to any lengths to win something for this club and that he could be trusted to deliver on the big occasion. It was great seeing him play so well in such a big match. He showed what talent he had and what a massive star he could be – even, as Mancini had claimed, to the extent that he might one day be one of the best three players in the world.'

Even Stoke manager Tony Pulis accepted that his team were well beaten on the day. He said, 'We are all desperately disappointed because today we didn't reach the level of performance we have over the last few months. It hurts to say this but Manchester City were the better team on the day and deserved to win. A few of our players were a little bit out of their depth at the end. But when you see that they had a £30m player on the bench and didn't even use him, you can see the difference between the two clubs.'

Sir Richard Leese, leader of Manchester City Council,

added to the congratulations but then put a dampener on it for City fans by also saluting United who had won the title with games to spare, 'City winning the FA Cup is a joyous occasion for many people in Manchester, myself included. Manchester United winning their 19th top flight title is a remarkable and historic achievement. Manchester's football clubs are a huge source of pride, helping to project the city's name around the world. It's only fitting that we host a public celebration of those achievements so fans can share the moment and enjoy the success. We expect some unforgettable scenes as fans gather to acclaim their team.'

But Patrick Vieira brought it back to what mattered for City fans – their own team's triumph – when he said, 'It means a lot to the players but even more to the fans. They have been waiting a long time for this. It is fantastic. There has been a lot of pressure on this team. It's a really fantastic season for us.

Meanwhile, Balotelli was in fine form, I am told, as the City camp celebrated their victory with a post-match meal at their hotel, the 5-star Grove in leafy Hertfordshire. 'Even in the dressing room and on the way back to the Grove in the coach Mario was in a very buoyant mood,' I am told. 'He was larking about in the dressing room with the cup and making the other players laugh as he messed about. He was delighted to have helped bring the cup back to Manchester and saw it as a thank you to the City fans who had backed him as he struggled to settle in Manchester.'

It appears Balotelli spent his meal talking to the waitresses and making them laugh and then led the way for a post-match swim celebration, where he and some other jokers jumped up and down clapping and shouting, 'We've won the cup' in the hotel's pool. 'He's just a great guy,' I am told. 'Nothing like the sulky bloke you might sometimes imagine – that's just down to his shyness. Mario is very generous, very kind and always makes time to talk to all the staff at the club. He was certainly friendly and polite to the staff and those who were staying at the Grove.'

It was the side of the boy most people never see – the side of the boy some people don't want to see, or acknowledge, because it would wreck the image of Mario as a madman who has little time for anyone but himself. But that night after the Wembley triumph for City best illustrated the person his friends, family and many at his football club know well – a warm, kind, generous lad who will go out of the way to make others feel wanted and liked. At the end of his first season at City, Mario could look back with some pride at helping the club to that FA Cup win and his goals tally. He had made 28 appearances for the club, scoring ten goals – but on the deficit side of the balance sheet, he accrued more yellow cards than goals...a total of 11...and had also been sent off twice.

So the promise was clearly there, but so was the hot-headed folly that could spell problems for both the players and the club. His challenge for his second season at the club would, clearly, be to keep up the good work with the goals and his contributions in key matches, but also to get a grip on that temper of his. It would be a challenge that would define his future at City. Before we analyse that second season, let's take a look at the footballers who had trodden the path that Mario had followed to Manchester – the Italian stallions who had laid the groundwork in the Premier League for the boy who would be the best of them all.

CHAPTER ELEVEN

ITALIAN STALLIONS

Of course, Mario wasn't the first Italian superstar to make it in the English Premier League. The trail was blazed by some players who would become legends – like Gianluca Vialli and Gianfranco Zola – and some who would fail to settle and make an impact and exit virtually as anonymously as they arrived. Indeed, the first Italian to ever play in the Premier League would fall into that rather sad category.

Andrea Silenzi arrived at Nottingham Forest in the summer of 1995 as one of the feted signings of manager Frank Clark. The Italian cost what was then a hefty fee of £1.8million from Torino. Silenzi was brought in as a like for like replacement for Stan Collymore, who had left the City Ground a few weeks earlier to join Liverpool for a then British transfer record of £8.5million. But the centre forward turned out to be a disaster – he just wasn't cut out for the hectic nature of British football with his overtly laid-back, languid style. In fact, some pundits and Forest fans wondered aloud if he was cut out for any type of football – and wondered how he had had such a seemingly garlanded career in Italy for the previous 11 years!

Silenzi had seemingly cut it at five other clubs before Forest were landed with him – including major outfits like Torino and Napoli. Silenzi even played up front with the legendary Diego Maradona at Napoli before moving to Torino. In his second season with Torino his two goal haul in the final helped his new club win the Italian FA Cup for the fourth time in their history as they outplayed Roma.

But there was never any indication that he would help deliver the same sort of glory to the City Ground – and the fans quickly tired of him. He stayed just over one season at Forest before being shipped out for good by new boss Dave Beasant, who was never impressed by his ability or attitude. In total, Silenzi made only 20 appearances (seven starts) for Forest, scoring just twice – once in the FA Cup against Oxford United and once in the League Cup against Bradford City.

The fans and the Press were relieved to see the back of him. Reuters' Patrick Johnston described his time at Forest in this way, 'Known affectionately as the Big Brush, Silenzi is was the first Italian to appear in the Premier League when he arrived in 1995 at a cost of 2.65 million euros, but he managed just two goals in his 20 games against the formidable Bradford and Oxford in cup competitions. He left, having had his contract torn up by manager Dave Bassett, for the sanctuary of Reggina two seasons later.'

The *Guardian*'s David Hills chose him as No 3 when the

paper did a 'Top Ten Worst Foreign Buyers Ever in the Premier League' in 2000. Hills commented, 'Earning a then-enormous £30,000 a month, his laid-back control, finishing and approach play soon had management and supporters worried. His only excess was in the length of his first touch. It took just weeks for the deal to look suspect, a month for it to look plain wrong and another to collapse. Half way through his first season, he had lost his place to Jason Lee, was loaned to Venezia, and when told to return by Dave Bassett, refused. Forest tore up his contract – meaning the whole deal, including wages and bonuses, had cost the club £2.75m. "The whole business turned into a complete fiasco," said Bassett.'

Noel Draper of football website The Daisy Cutter also made the valid point that not only did Silenzi's flop reflect badly upon him, it also helped get Frank Clark the sack, 'Frank Clark, the then manager of Nottingham Forest, paid £1.8 million for the services of Andrea Silenzi in 1995. What he had hoped he had signed was a tall centre forward with an eye for a goal. What he actually got was a tall centre forward with an eye for a nice wage. At the time, £30,000 pounds a month was a huge salary, especially for an unproven journeyman from Italy. Bemused by the signing but still trusting the wisdom of their manager, Forest fans gave Andrea the benefit of the doubt. Within a few games they began to wish they hadn't. Silenzi was a 6ft 3in forward with a bad touch, poor finishing and non-existent build up play. Forest fans and the Forest board were appalled by Clark's judgment and the signing of Silenzi contributed to his removal as the manager.'

Another disaster from Italy was Manchester United keeper

Massimo Taibi. It isn't that often that Sir Alex Ferguson drops a clanger when splashing out for new talent but when he does – yes, I'm thinking of you, Bebe, and you, Juan Veron! – he does it big-time. Veron set United back a then record British record fee of £28.1million in 2001 but failed to make a regular impact. But if it is any consolation to the Argentine midfielder, the Italian Taibi was even worse! He was snapped up from Venezia for £4.5million – to replace United's greatest ever keeper, Peter Schmeichel. The great Dane had bowed out after winning the Champions League in May 1999 and Taibi arrived a few months later. The BBC reported the signing at the time, pointing out Taibi was experienced and was expected to challenge Mark Bosnich for the No 1 spot at the club, 'Taibi, who has joined United in a deal which is worth a reported £4.5m, has signed a four-year contract. The 29-year-old keeper completed a medical at Old Trafford on Tuesday before heading back to Italy. He will be back in Manchester later this week where he will be unveiled at a media conference. United boss Sir Alex Ferguson has moved for Taibi to increase competition among his goalkeepers. Ferguson has turned to 36-year-old Dutchman Raimond van der Gouw to cover for the injured Mark Bosnich but now has three experienced keepers to choose from.'

Fergie had been unhappy with Bosnich, but would end up even more frustrated by Taibi as he tried desperately to plug the gap left by the virtually irreplaceable Schmeichel. Taibi ended up playing only four matches for the Red Devils – including a 5-0 defeat by Chelsea. Just a couple of months after his arrival he was gone, back to Italy on loan – and would eventually sign for Reggina for £2.5million. He was ultimately seen as a figure of fun – with one paper famously dubbing him 'The Blind Venetian' – although my view is that he didn't really stand a chance. No one could have replaced Schmeichel at the time...he was THAT good.

Fergie himself realised that was the case and eventually went out and bought the only keeper on the planet who could show his medals and lay claim to being the new No 1 keeper in the world. Yes, French World Cup winner Fabien Barthez arrived at Old Trafford in 2000 to finally replace Schmeichel (and, let's be honest, even he wasn't really in Peter's league!). The ave.it.net website summed up the way Taibi was seen as he eventually returned to Italy for good, 'Sir Alex signed him to replace Peter Schmeichel? In 1999, with Raimond van der Gouw always wearing his bridesmaid's outfit and Mark Bosnich too cocky by half, Sir Alex Ferguson splashed out £4.5m on Venezia journeyman Massimo Taibi. The omnipresent tracksuit bottoms should have caused Ferguson to pause for thought. Instead, Taibi conceded two sloppy goals at Liverpool on his debut and one to Wimbledon the following week. Then the fun began: Southampton scored three at Old Trafford, including a Matthew Le Tissier "shot" that trickled through Taibi's legs and was so soft, it barely crossed the line. Eight days later, Chelsea put five past him at Stamford Bridge and this Italian's job was over, little more than a month after it had begun. Taibi rotted in the reserves until Reggina took him on loan before a £2.5m purchase at season's end. He was, noted a generous Roy Keane, "clearly a good keeper". Clearly.'

Having seen Taibi suffer I was pleased for him when he regained some of his credibility at Reggina – especially when he scored for them in the Serie A match at home to Udinese in the 2000/01 season, when they had been losing 1-0! The so-called clown had the last laugh...

But while there were a few flops from Italy in our top-flight, there were many more players who arrived and left behind a lasting impression for their obvious talent and craft.

Arguably the best of the lot was the wonderful Gianfranco Zola – who starred for Chelsea from 1996 to 2003. He joined the Blues for a fee of £4.5million under the continuing foreign revolution implemented at the club by then boss Ruud Gullit. Zola wore the No 25 shirt and would become a hero among the Chelsea fans for his intelligent play and passion for the cause. Zola was signed from Parma but was probably best remembered in Italy for his time at Napoli, when he initially played understudy to Maradona and then took on his role when the Argentine genius left.

'I learnt everything from Diego,' Zola would later admit. 'I used to spy on him every time he trained and learned how to curl a free-kick just like him. After one year I had completely changed. I saw him do things in training and in matches I had never even dreamed possible. He was simply the best I've ever seen. I'm not saying I wouldn't have been a good player if I had not played with him at that stage of my career but I do know I wouldn't be the player I am now.'

With Maradona gone, Zola became the main man for a couple of seasons in Naples before then joining Parma, where he helped them win the UEFA Cup. But when Carlo Ancelotti joined as manager, he decided Zola did not fit into his plans and put him up for sale. Aged 30, Zola could have wondered who would now have faith in him. He needn't have worried as Gullit came in and bought him; the Dutch master instinctively recognising the quality and experience the little Sardinian could bring to his team. Gullit would now build the team around Zola.

In the autumn of his career, the Italian now produced his best football and found his true spiritual home. He would stay at Chelsea for seven seasons, scored 80 goals and was voted Premier League Player of the Year in 1997. Finally, at the age of 37 he decided it was time to return home to Italy and ended his career at Cagliari.

In 2003 Chelsea's fans voted him the greatest player ever to wear the blue of Chelsea – a remarkable achievement when you consider he was up against stars including the legendary Peter Osgood. In turn, Zola would eventually admit that of all the stops on his wonderful footballing career – also including Napoli and Cagliari – he enjoyed his time at the Bridge most of all, 'The team where I had the best time of my career.'

The official Chelsea website, www.chelseafc.com, would sum up his time at the Bridge in this way, 'Over seven seasons Gianfranco Zola captivated Chelsea supporters to the extent that he was twice made Player of the Year and in 2003 was voted as the club's greatest ever player, receiving 60% of the votes in a poll on Chelsea's official website. He helped win four trophies and scored the winner in the 1998 European Cup Winners' Cup Final just seconds after coming on as substitute. In all Franco, scored 80 goals in 312 games, with many of them being spectacular efforts.

'Goals that will live long in the memory include the mid-air back flick against Norwich City, an effort against Manchester United that left opposition goalkeeper Peter Schmeichel motionless and a brilliant turn and shot in the 1997 FA Cup semi-final win over Wimbledon. Above all,

Franco always played football as if he enjoyed it and was almost universally popular amongst opposition fans.'

The BBC succinctly detailed that winning strike in the 1998 Cup Winners' Cup Final, 'Gianfranco Zola was the hero as Chelsea won the European Cup Winners' Cup 1-0 against Stuttgart in Stockholm. He had been on the pitch for barely 30 seconds when Dennis Wise clipped the ball into space down the Chelsea left. At once, Zola was away, skating clear of the Stuttgart back line as he sped into the box. As goalkeeper Franz Wohlfahrt came off his line, Zola unleashed a guided missile with his right foot that screamed past the Austrian and into the roof of the net. It was Zola's fourth goal in the competition and his 12th of the season.'

Former Blues chairman Ken Bates had no doubt that Zola had earned his place in the elite annals of the club. 'Zola was undoubtedly one of Chelsea's greatest players ever,' he told Channel 4's Football Italia. 'He's been a joy to watch and a great influence both on and off the field, particularly because of his great interest with young fans. We owe him a hell of a lot of thanks.'

Zola himself was delighted with the accolades from the fans, the people whom, in his always modest, always humble, opinion, mattered most. He would say, 'My greatest satisfaction is off the pitch for the way people consider me and the respect they give me. Many people excel in games but when you have achieved that level of respect it is something special. Money can give you many things but respect cannot be bought. What I have achieved in the way people regard me, in my mind, is remarkable.'

If we are agreed on Zola being the greatest Italian ever to grace the Prem, the man who shared much of the glory with him in later years at the Bridge can't be that far behind. Yes, step forward into the limelight Gianluca Vialli. As both a player and manager at the Bridge, Vialli also earned his place in the club's book of legends.

Like Zola, Vialli signed up at Chelsea in 1996 from Juventus, where he had been a champion and a hero. He left the club on the biggest high – captaining the side that won the Champions League by beating Ajax Amsterdam 4-2 on penalties in the final after the match itself had ended 1-1.

He arrived in London on a salary reputed to be around £1million a year and showed why as he helped the team win the FA Cup in his first season as they beat Middlesbrough 2-0 at Wembley. But he and boss Gullit endured a fractious relationship and Vialli was hardly a regular choice by the time Gullit was dismissed in February 1998.

But it was to Vialli that the Blues' board would turn when it came to a replacement for the fallen Dutchman – and he gladly took up the gauntlet as the club's player-manager.

BBC Sport was one of many organisations to express surprise at the choice, 'A year ago, Gianluca Vialli cut a sorry figure left on the bench, rebelliously smoking cigarettes, as Ruud Gullit took Chelsea to Wembley and beyond. The Italian was furious at his lack of opportunity, but there were clear signs earlier this season that he had taken a more responsible attitude. Out went the fags and veiled criticisms of Gullit, in came a determination to do all he could to win a place in the starting line-up, and to accept without complaint when he was dropped. It must have impressed the powers-that-be at Chelsea, but even so their choice of him as a replacement for Gullit is a huge surprise.'

A shock maybe, but within just over a year the Italian had

won three trophies! Under his guidance Chelsea triumphed in the League Cup, the European Cup Winners' Cup (thanks to compatriot Zola's winner) and the European Super Cup. The latter involved them beating Champions League winners Real Madrid. In those first two seasons in charge Vialli also took Chelsea to fourth and third place finishes in the Premier League.

He played his final game for the club in 1999 which meant he had made 88 appearances and scored 40 goals, not far off one every two games – and not at all bad when you consider his breakdown of relationship with Gullit meant he was in and out of the team during the latter end of the Dutchman's reign, so consistency of form was not easy to establish.

As manager, he also took the club to the last eight of the Champions League in 2000 where they were defeated by Barcelona and led them to an FA Cup Final win over Aston Villa at Wembley. At the start of the 2000/01 season he also led them to an FA Charity Shield win over Manchester United but he was sacked after a poor start to the league campaign and fallouts with several stars including Zola and the tough Frenchman Didier Deschamps.

It had been a shock that Vialli had been appointed manager in the first place. Now, after a surprising level of success that had seen him lift five trophies, it was a shock that he had been sacked. The *Independent* led the way in reporting his dismissal at the time, 'Gianluca Vialli was fired today as Chelsea's manager with the club saying in a statement he had been "released from his duties" immediately. Vialli, 36, who joined Chelsea in the summer of 1996 on a free transfer from Juventus, took over as player manager in 1998 after Ruud Gullit was fired. That season he guided Chelsea to the European Cup Winners Cup title and the domestic League Cup title. The club has won only one of its first five matches this season in the English Premier League with doubts its cosmopolitan side can compete with powers like Manchester United and Arsenal. In a statement, the west London club expressed admiration for Vialli's two and a half year reign but said in a "wider context it is in our best interests to seek a change of direction." No successor has yet been appointed and "for the immediate future" the current staff, led by coach Graham Rix, will take charge of the team.'

Vialli would now go off to manage Watford in the First Division – and eventually end up as a commentator on Sky Italia.

While we are concentrating on Chelsea, it makes sense to mention the third of the Italian triumvirate that took the club to such heights in the late nineties and early Noughties. Roberto di Matteo would be the man who would score the first goal for the club in the 2-0 FA Cup Final win over Middlesbrough in 1997. It was the same match in which his friend Zola played – and that goal itself went down in history as the fastest goal (42 seconds) ever scored in an FA Cup Final at the old Wembley. Di Matteo was born in Switzerland to Italian parents, but he always made it clear he saw himself as an Italian. Indeed he was capped 34 times for Italy and scored two goals for the national side. And he came to Chelsea's attention specifically because of his exploits with Rome giants Lazio, with whom he starred from 1993 to 1996.

In '96 he was snapped up by Ruud Gullit for Chelsea for a then club record fee of £4.9million. As well as the FA Cup, he helped the Blues win the European Cup Winners' Cup and the League Cup. He became part of a formidable four-man midfield at the Bridge along with Dennis Wise, Gus Poyet and Dan Petrescu. In 2000 he scored again at Wembley as Chelsea beat Aston Villa to win the FA Cup, this time his goal came on 70 minutes and was the winner as Chelsea emerged triumphant 1-0. Not only that, but Di Matteo made history yet again – his goal was the final one scored in the FA Cup at the old Wembley. Soon the stadium would be knocked down with a new one rising in its place.

Di Matteo would admit his sadness at its demise, saying, 'It's a shame they're tearing the old place down – it has been a very lucky ground for me.'

Two years later, in February 2002, his Chelsea dream would come to an end when he was forced to retire at the age of 31. Eighteen months earlier he had suffered a triple fracture in a Uefa Cup game against Swiss side St Gallen. Di Matteo said at the time: 'I have worked hard to try and get back but unfortunately I am still experiencing problems and I have had to face up to the sad decision that my playing days are over. I have loved my time at Chelsea and I am glad to have played my part in bringing success to the club and the fans, who have always been great to me.'

Club managing director Colin Hutchinson was just as saddened by his demise, saying: 'This is devastating news and we feel for Roberto. He has worked long and hard to try and get back playing. He has endured a series of painful operations and slogged away on the training ground but cruelly the injury has beaten him.'

Beaten maybe, but not out for the count. No, Di Matteo would show some of the fighting qualities that made him such a competitive, class midfielder by now moving into management. He would do a good job at MK Dons, so good in fact that West Bromwich Albion would come calling for him. He took the Baggies up to the Premier League from the Championship but would then be sacked five months later as Albion went through a rough patch. Chairman Jeremy Peace said it was not a move he relished, adding, 'On behalf of the board, I would like to thank Roberto for his efforts over the past 19 months, particularly for his contribution towards last season's promotion success and our very promising start to the current campaign. We wish him and his family well for the future. 'Roberto embraced the structure in which we wanted him to work and he has been a good colleague. However, we are in a results-driven industry and felt we had no choice but to act now.'

Roberto stayed silent but the fans spoke out on his behalf. They were stunned at the decision after the job the Italian had done at the Hawthorns. 'Just who the hell do WBA think they are?' asked one. 'They have serious delusions of grandeur if they expect to finish anywhere above the bottom 6 in the Premier League in their first season back. RDM is one of the best up and coming managers around and was working on a shoestring. As per usual the owners expect too much and panic and good people pay the price. It's to be hoped that RDM will get another chance with a club more worthy of his undoubted managerial talent. As for the Baggies, they deserve all they get...and that will no doubt be relegation, then they can sack RDM's replacement!'

While another added, 'What exactly were the WBA board expecting to achieve in their first season after promotion? I can't help but think they have made a huge mistake. But for dodgy refereeing decisions they would be safe by now. Even now they are still not in the relegation places. Absolute joke!'

Di Matteo would get another chance to prove himself – and, ironically, it would come after another manager was sacked. In 2011, he became assistant to Andre Villas Boas when the Portuguese took over at Roberto's old club, Chelsea. But when Villas Boas was sacked in March 2012, Roberto took over the reins as a caretaker manager until the end of the season.

Under his more stable stewardship, results improved dramatically as the Blues headed for a Champions League semi-final with Barcelona. They had lost 3-1 in Napoli under Villas Boas but Di Matteo engineered a remarkable comeback – as Chelsea thrashed Maradona's former club 4-1 in the return at the Bridge. He then masterminded their win over Benfica in the quarter finals while also leading them to an FA Cup semi-final against Tottenham after they crushed Leicester 5-2 in the last eight. And of course, Di Matteo also guided Chelsea to their first Champions League win, over Bayern Munich in May 2012, only to be sacked the following November.

But it wasn't just at Stamford Bridge that the Italian pioneers prospered. Another of Gianluca Vialli's old mates would light up the north east of England during the 1990s. Fabrizio Ravanelli, who won the Champions League in the same Juventus side as Vialli in 1996. Indeed it was Ravanelli who scored the Boro goal in normal time, before the match went to penalties.

After that glorious triumph, Ravanelli, like Vialli, left Juventus and head for England. But while Vialli ended up at the Bridge, Ravanelli joined Bryan Robson's Middlesbrough revolution in the industrial heartlands of the north east. He cost £7million and received a warm welcome from the fans at the Riverside (as well as a £1.3million a year, four-year deal). Robson justified the signing, saying, 'You have to spend a lot of money to get this type of player'. He also insisted that the Italian was one of the world's top four strikers.

The *Independent* superbly summed up what his signing meant to Boro and English football generally at the time, 'The arrival of Fabrizio Ravanelli at Middlesbrough for £7million yesterday was another pointer to the growing power of the Premiership on both the home front and in Europe. At 27, the silver-haired Italian international is a gilt-edged striker, who may have been surplus to requirements at over-staffed Juventus, but was coveted by other Italian clubs. That he chose the Premiership - along with a string of other front-line players in what is turning out to be a golden summer for overseas signings – shows that the game here is now operating on the same exalted level as Serie A – the big-money league of Europe.

'Two years ago Ravanelli swapping Turin for Teesside would have been laughed at. Then came the Brazilians Juninho and Branco, coupled with a new stadium, a flood of cash from a share of satellite television with pots more to come, and Middlesbrough start looking less like Hartlepool United and more like Manchester United.'

And Ravanelli's career at Boro couldn't have got off to a better start – he grabbed a hat-trick on his league debut against Liverpool on the opening day of the 1996/97 season. But it turned sour – largely because the wins dried up and Ravanelli himself turned sour. He did himself no favours by moaning about the city, the weather and the training facilities at the club.

In a topsy-turvy season, Boro were relegated the season he joined but he helped take them to the finals of the FA Cup and the League Cup. Unfortunately, they lost both – 2-0 to Chelsea in the FA Cup at Wembley and 1-0 to Leicester in the League Cup final replay at Hillsborough. In the first match at Wembley Ravanelli earned Boro their replay when he put them ahead in the 95th minute, only for Emile Heskey to equalise.

In the replay, Boro simply could not find the back of the net and Steve Claridge's goal in extra time won it for the Foxes. His travels would then take him on to Marseilles and Lazio in Rome, but he would return to England in 2001 when Derby County took a punt on his service. Memorably, he arrived with his advisers at the club, all in sunglasses and sharp suits and the Press made the astute comment that they looked as if they were heading for the set of Reservoir Dogs! The Mail announced his arrival at the club, 'Fabrizio Ravanelli ended weeks of speculation yesterday when he promised to sign for Derby tomorrow. The former Italy striker decided on the move after meeting Lazio general director Massimo Cragnotti yesterday at the club's training camp in Riscone Di Brunico. He said: "I am going to Derby and I am looking forward to joining them. I will go there on Friday to sign a contract but it is still to be decided whether it is for two or three years." The former Juventus frontman, 32, who scored eight goals in 22 appearances for Italy, still had two years left on his contract at Lazio. It appears he reached a compromise with Cragnotti, clearing the way for his return.'

But by November 2001, with Derby languishing at the bottom of the Premiership, Ravanelli was talking publicly about how he now regretted having left Lazio. 'Now the coach is Alberto Zaccheroni at Lazio and, with him, maybe I would have the possibility to play more,' Ravanelli said, in an interview with website Planet Football. 'Of course, I am still in contact with the guys back there. They tell me about Zaccheroni, about his attacking tactics. Who knows how many games I would have played?'

It was an echo of his time at Boro when he complained out loud although, to give him his due, the Italian did his best to save Derby from the drop. But, ultimately, he was unable to do it on his own and the club were relegated in 2002 and by 2003 Ravanelli would be gone from English football for good.

But the website forzaitalianfootball.com made the claim – substantiated by several fans of Boro and County that I have spoken to – that there remains a fondness at the two clubs for the Italian, 'Although his 2 seasons in the Premier League have ended in relegation he is still a well-loved figure at the two clubs. Recently he expressed a desire to be at Middlesbrough again, but this time as manager. 31 goals in 84 appearances for struggling clubs showed his ability to find the net and added with his "shirt over the head" celebrations has secured him a place in Premiership folklore.'

Another Italian who would earn hero status in England was the fiery Paolo Di Canio. He played for Italian giants Lazio, Milan, Napoli and Juventus before arriving in the UK with Glasgow Celtic in 1996. He spent a year in Scotland and then began his odyssey in England with Sheffield Wednesday. He became the Premier League's most controversial Italian import before Balotelli, making headlines as much for his controversial exploits as his undoubted talents. He was the Balotelli prototype as he clashed with his own team-mates and officials. His moment of greatest infamy came in September 1998, when he pushed referee Paul Alcock to the ground after being sent off while playing for Wednesday against Arsenal at Hillsborough. The incident led to him being fined £10,000 and banned for 11 matches.

The ban – which included a three-match suspension for the sending off and another eight matches for the push – meant Di Canio would not play for the club again from the end of October in 1998 until almost the end of the year. Afterwards a contrite Di Canio announced, 'I want to say that I'm very, very sorry for what's happened. I had a fair hearing. I'll see the Sheffield Wednesday fans on Boxing Day, the first game after my suspension.' The FA's director of public affairs, David Davies, said, 'Following the hearing, the commission was unanimous that an urgent recommendation should go to the FA's disciplinary committee to ask that it should be made clear to all concerned that stronger penalties should be imposed immediately on any player who manhandles a match official.'

Di Canio would also be accused of far Right views during his career but, like Balotelli, he had another side to his character. That side saw him win the Scottish Player of the Year award in 1997 and a FIFA Fair Play Award four years later. The latter honour came his way while he was at West Ham. The London *Evening Standard* explained why he had been honoured – and how it represented a turnaround in the player's fortunes, 'Paolo Di Canio today won FIFA's prestigious fair play award for his amazing act of sportsmanship during West Ham's Premiership clash with Everton last December. It is a remarkable achievement for a player who, until the incident at Goodison Park, was better known for his temperamental behaviour and the 11-match ban he served for pushing over referee Paul Alcock in 1998. But FIFA's fair play committee, meeting here ahead of Saturday's World Cup draw, decided past reputations counted for nothing and rewarded the West Ham player for his sporting gesture. Di Canio won the award, which will be presented to him next month by last year's winner, Lucas Radebe, of Leeds, for spurning the chance to score while Everton keeper Paul Gerrard was lying injured with a dislocated knee.

'With the scores level at 1-1, Di Canio had a chance to win the match but instead caught the ball in the penalty area, allowing Gerrard to receive treatment. The Premiership has already given Di Canio a fair play award and earlier this year Gerrard presented Di Canio with a special framed photograph to say thank you for his unselfish act. Now FIFA have followed suit by giving him worldwide recognition.'

FIFA Director of communications Keith Cooper said: 'His past reputation didn't come into it at all and those people who know Paolo Di Canio will tell you he never deserved it anyway. This gesture was taken on its own merits. People like him who are impetuous are as likely to do something very honourable as they are to do something dishonourable. 'There is often a lot of criticism of people like him when they do something bad, so why not honour people when they do something good.

'One or two of the committee members already knew about Di Canio's gesture before today. One of the features of the Premiership is it is widely watched. What he did will have been seen in many countries around the world.'

Paul Gerrard himself had said: 'I was genuinely injured and Paolo realised that. He has a reputation as a controversial character but I owe him a thank-you for what he did. I have never experienced anything like that before. When you are on the pitch you do everything you can to win but Paolo put my welfare first and I appreciate that.'

His four years at West Ham, from 1999–2003, were the highlight of his career in England and he admitted he had a special love for the club – which was certainly reciprocated by the fans. He then had a season with Charlton before returning to Lazio. But he would never forget his time in England, particularly at West Ham.

In March, 2008, Di Canio announced his retirement from football after a 23-year playing career and began coaching lessons. Soon he revealed that he wanted to move into club management and that his dream was to become boss at West Ham. Before moving back to England as Swindon manager, he would admit, 'I believe my future will be in England. In the next few days something will happen, perhaps in an inferior division. English football is loyal, full of pride and I believe I'm close to returning to England. It is the country that I most love from a football standpoint. I am very saddened by West Ham's relegation. This team has always been in my heart. They have unique supporters. I would give everything for West Ham. I even have a Hammers tattoo.'

In 2010, West Ham had honoured the Italian by opening the 'Paolo Di Canio Lounge', within the West Stand of the Boleyn Ground. Di Canio had been in attendance on the big day, unveiling a plaque to commemorate it. Di Canio would say, 'You can't imagine how I feel. It is always an emotional moment when I come back, but today is even more a special occasion. To be here for this opening of a new lounge that has been given in my name has made me proud. It is a great honour to be here, to meet the fans and to stay close with this club.

'I can only say thanks to everyone to everybody and whenever I can, I will come back to the lounge because this stadium is my second home. The very first members of my lounge will always be special to me. It is beautiful, trendy and has style. When I go back to Italy, I will be glad to think that lots of fans are here and looking at me as a player who gave something to this club. To know that my link with this club will remain is fantastic.'

The move highlighted the love-in between the club, the club's fans and the man himself – and led many pundits to speculate just how long it would be before the Italian was anointed manager at Upton Park.

But first he would have to serve a tough apprenticeship in the lower leagues to prove to the Board that he was capable of being trusted with the job. The man who would be the predecessor for Balotelli in England had a tough grounding. Recently he has been making a name for himself as a manager – at Swindon Town in League Two, and doing a good job in his first role in charge. He took the club to the final of the Football League Trophy at Wembley, where they lost 2-0 to Chesterfield, but also led them on a promotion charge. Typically, his stint at the club has not been without controversy! He was appointed to the post in May 2011 after the Robins had been relegated to League Two and the following August was involved in a pitch-side row with his own striker Leon Clarke, after they had lost in the League Cup to Southampton. Sky summed it up, saying, 'Swindon manager Paolo Di Canio could be in trouble after getting into a fight with one of his players. The Italian got into an argument with striker Leon Clarke as he left the pitch after Swindon's 3-1 defeat to Southampton in the Carling Cup. Footage of the incident shows Di Canio trying to push Clarke towards the tunnel.

'The pair are then seen shoving each other before club staff and stewards intervene. The brawl continued into the tunnel after the game. Following the bust-up, Clarke refused to go into the dressing room and left the ground still wearing his kit, while Di Canio left without attending the post-match news conference.' Swindon chairman Jeremy Wray pledged to get to the bottom of the matter, saying, 'Leon and the fitness coach were having words after the game and there was a disagreement between them. As Leon came off the pitch Paolo was conscious these things should be done behind closed doors. There was a misunderstanding there that carried on into the tunnel. It got to a situation where the whole thing blew up very fast. There was frustration on both sides.'

But Wray backed the manager and Di Canio refused to back down, promising that Clarke would never play for the club while he was in charge. The Italian kept to his word: Clarke was loaned out to Chesterfield and Crawley Town.

Di Canio also proved he can cut it as a manger by inspiring Swindon to beat Premier League Wigan Athletic, 2-1 at home in the FA Cup 3rd Round in January 2012. The win meant they had reached the 4th Round for the first time since 1996 and Di Canio was typically buoyant and full of hyperbole afterwards. He said, 'My lads today deserve to have their names put on this stadium. I know you normally do this when you win something important and I don't want a big statue but maybe a plaque. Today we did something special. There is no doubt we deserved to win. It is the best moment of my life. Today they did show the dream can come true. We needed to limit Wigan's chances to get through and we did that well apart from the accident for the penalty. This is something special - an amazing performance against a team three divisions above us. The players have been fantastic because to play under me is difficult.' He also dedicated the win to his father, who died late in 2011.

It was honest of him to acknowledge that playing under him was 'difficult'. He was a hard task master and demanded his men gave everything all the time. He was also still combustible with officialdom – not long after the win over Wigan, he was sent to the stands by the referee after complaining about a decision in the league clash with Macclesfield.

It was his third indiscretion of the season but he was defiant afterwards, saying that he would not change his ways, 'I did not swear or say any bad words but the referee sent me off because he did not like my body language. I am a passionate man and if I want to wave my arms in the air nobody is going to stop me. If the FA charge me I will appeal because if I deserved to be sent off for that I will be in the stands every week. If they send me off 25 times it does not matter because I have a great team and we will still win the league.'

Certainly the fans loved him – and not just at Swindon. Over at his old club West Ham, they were consistently chanting his name and calling for him to replace Sam

Allardyce during the final months of the season in 2012. And while some fans across the UK were busy criticising Di Canio for his outbursts, fans at Swindon and West Ham were busy defending him. One Hammers fan said, 'Stop moaning about PDC – just accept him warts and all. He's ace and is a future manager of West Ham.' While a Swindon fan commented, 'I have Italian background and if you asked me to express myself without moving my arms, then you might as well cut them off as this is what we do! The English game is getting so painfully political it is squeezing what life we have left in this once beautiful game. Wake up and let Paolo express himself, as he is doing no one any harm is he? The ref was an absolute disgrace that day and this summed up his afternoon when he sent our God into the stands. BRAVO DI CANIO. Don't change for no one (and hands off you Hammers as you are doin' alright with Allardyce). Swindon is the hand & PDC is our glove!' They were strong words of defence for a strong character who you either loved or hated – just like Balotelli. As Di Canio continued to divide opinions in England after so many years in the country, so did Mario after just a couple of seasons. Both men were passionate Italians with a fiery nature but also had a good side. As Mario spent a lot of time with disadvantaged children and the poor, so Paolo also supported charitable causes – without blowing his own trumpet publicly as did many footballers.

There was another controversial Italian footballer trying his luck in England before Balotelli – but he could in no way claim to have been as successful as Di Canio or Mario...or even successful at all. His name was Marco Materazzi, a defender who joined Everton. He would last just one season at Goodison. The Everton website toffeeweb commented,

'Marco Materazzi is a tall, mobile and aggressive player who should have suited English football. He became the first Italian to play for Everton...The initial assessment of Materazzi by Evertonians was not so glowing: He was a bit of a disappointment on the pre-season tour of Holland and Belgium. He was slow on the turn and when starting to run, though once he got into his stride those long legs give him fair pace...But as the season progressed, reports soon began to improve...But his downside was poor discipline. And an annoying tendency for getting himself sent off. Sadly, murmurings of unrest surrounded Mazza as his first season in England ended; his days at Goodison were already numbered. Citing personal reasons and inability to settle on Merseyside.'

It was a succinct summary by an excellent fans' website.

The *Guardian* also made the point that he had not lived up to his billing, 'Materazzi had arrived at Goodison Park from Perugia in 1998 when the then manager Walter Smith convinced his board he was buying a centre-half of immense potential. Unfortunately it remained untapped. "Materazzi got booked 12 times and sent off three times during his season at Everton so it all turned out a bit chaotic for him and everyone else," said Barry Horne yesterday. "Playing-wise our paths just missed crossing but, even though I'd moved on by the time he joined, I remained an Everton fan and kept in touch with my old team-mates. I certainly don't remember too many Everton players I talked to suggesting Materazzi had untapped potential or latent talent..."'

Of course, the man dubbed 'a lunatic' by many during his one and only season in England would fully live up to his name in the 2006 World Cup final between Italy and France (which Italy won on penalties) – when he was involved in an incident which ended with a disgraceful head-butt on him by Zinedine Zidane. The Frenchman was playing his last match as a professional but saw red after head-butting the Italian defender in the chest during extra time. Materazzi had apparently made a remark after the France legend complained the Inter Milan centre-back had pulled his shirt throughout the game.

It is the incident that the Italian will always be remembered for – as well as those three red cards at Everton! As the Bleacher Report's Tommy Nolan once said, 'Marco Materazzi joined Everton from Perugia in 1998-99. Materazzi's stay in the Premiership was brief and not so glorious after he became Walter Smith's first signing for Everton from Perugia in the summer of 1998. Materazzi's most famous moment at Everton was when he was sent off against Coventry after he was the victim of a Darren Huckerby dive. In that single season Materazzi managed to clock up three red cards and 12 yellows. He rejoined Perugia in the summer of 1999.'

It was a route many pundits in Italy believed Mario himself was destined to follow, given his volatile temperament. City fans had seen both sides to the boy during his first season at the club – but they loved him as he helped them lift the FA Cup. Now they were praying that Balotelli would not let the red mist destroy him in his second season. If he could control his temper, City could surely make a proper go of winning the Premier League. Then Mario would truly be assured of legendary status at the club – for ever.

CHAPTER TWELVE

SEEING RED

'The problem is because of his age, he can make some mistakes. He's Mario. He's crazy – but I love him because he's a good guy.'

Roberto Mancini, October 2011

MARIO's second season at City would see him aiming to help the club win their first top-flight league title since 1968 – but would also see him continually still questioned over his attitude and temperament. Luckily for the Italian, the man who mattered most in his career in England continued to stand by him and defend him, even when it seemed the whole world of football might be against him.

Yes, Mario was undoubtedly fortunate to have Roberto Mancini remain in his corner, fighting for him and defending him. The City manager's opinion was succinctly summed up by his quote at the start of this chapter: he still believed that

Mario could be one of the world's footballing greats, but he also understood that he was really still a boy. That he was having to mature and grew up in public and, given the enormity of the press focus on him, he deserved to be cut a little slack if and when he made a mistake.

Mario was raring to go when the 2011/12 campaign got underway with the traditional season curtain-raiser, the Community Shield, which is played at Wembley. City were contesting the shield in its current form for the first time – and their bow in the event could not have been tastier or more guaranteed to persuade them to take it seriously. Yes, their rivals at the national stadium would be Manchester United. City were there as FA Cup winners; United as Premier League winners...the latter being the title that all City fans most craved and one that the club under Mancini would be particularly concentrating their efforts in the campaign that was to follow.

Mario lasted just under an hour of the match before he was replaced by Gareth Barry and City would lose 3-2 after leading 2-0 at half time. Mario, like many of the players on display, looked a tad rusty and it was clear he would need to bed into the season and pick up his fitness. City had gone ahead through Joleon Lescott and Edin Dzeko. But a goal from Chris Smalling and a brace from Nani turned the tide. 'Maybe they played better than us,' Mancini said afterwards. 'But the right result after 90 minutes would probably have been 2-2. I am disappointed with the result, but it was the first game of the season, and anything can happen because all of the team are not in good form. We are disappointed but it is important we understand why we made the mistakes.'

City captain Vincent Kompany also felt that too much

should not be read into the result – and that it did not mean United would retain the title. He told talkSPORT, 'It would have been nice to win it, obviously, but the fact that we didn't win it is not going to change anything about how we work towards the Swansea game [the following Monday]. If anything it's good that we have another 90 minutes in our legs. It wasn't our best performance today but next week is going to be the big one. We've got a lot of potential so come the league, come the Champions League, come the FA Cup we'll be ready for it, there's no doubt about it.'

Mario was disappointed about losing to United, but he saw the defeat in the same light as Kompany; the result itself was not important, at least he had some time on the field under his belt as he tried to reach match fitness for the new season. But the Italian was disappointed when he now failed to get any playing time in City's next three games. He had worked hard for the Wembley curtain-raiser but then found himself on the bench as City won their first three Premier League fixtures in August 2011 (beating Swansea 4-0 at home, Bolton 3-2 away and Tottenham 5-1 away).

OK, the team had begun the campaign at a blistering pace and Sergio Aguero was quickly proving his worth upfront after his £35million move to City from Atletico Madrid in the summer. But Mario was itching to get out there and show the City fans that he was worth a place in the starting line-up, too.

His chance to shine finally came in City's home game in the league with Wigan on September 10. He came off the bench with 18 minutes to go and it would prove difficult to shine given that the man he replaced had already hit a hat-trick! Yes, Aguero was setting a scorching pace and fully justifying his status as the club's No 1 striker. For now, Mario would have to be patient: he would have to knuckle down and earn his place in the team and, hopefully, keep out of trouble away from the football field!

His chance did come – and he hit the ground running, just as Aguero had. On September 21, Aguero was given a night off (watching from the subs' bench) as City welcomed Birmingham for a Carling Cup 3rd Round match. City strolled to a 2-0 win with Owen Hargreaves and Mario earning the plaudits with a goal apiece and the Mail best summed up their efforts, 'Happily there was a rather sunnier tale to tell as Owen Hargreaves – he of much talent and little luck – returned to competitive football with a goal. He and Mario Balotelli put Birmingham to the sword, but on this occasion the Italy striker was never going to be the centre of discussion...Balotelli and Carlos Tevez both played 90 minutes. The former acquitted himself the better. The goal he scored was a good one and he also came close in the second half, curling a lovely shot towards goal from 20 yards only to see it land on the top of the net. Mancini has been pleased with Balotelli's attitude so far this season. There have been signs of maturity.'

Three days later Mario was back on the bench as Mancini paired Edin Dzeko with Aguero for the Premier League visit of Everton. Mario would replace the big Bosnian on the hour – and mark his appearance with another goal, his second in two games as City beat the Merseysiders 2-0. And this time he was the big hero as he broke the deadlock – and Everton's dogged resistance – with a goal just eight minutes after he appeared on the field of play. He was set up by Aguero and finished clinically before then heading to the touchline to embrace his manager! A late goal by James Milner clinched the win for City.

Afterwards Mancini appeared a mite embarrassed when asked how he felt about being embraced by his young countryman. He tried to explain it in this way, 'Sometimes when he scores, Mario is unhappy. Today, he was happy because he knew it was an important goal. His behaviour can be so-so, we know this. But Mario didn't play for four games and he has worked well and didn't say anything. He waited for this moment. He likes Manchester City, he likes English football and he can improve with the team.'

The *Sun* also praised Mario and pointed out that he would be missed in City's Champions League clash at Bayern Munich a couple of days later, 'His team-mates may think he's nuts – but they also know Mario Balotelli is a cracker. And how they could do with him tomorrow against a Bayern Munich side which have not conceded a goal in nine games this season. But the Italian bad-boy, 21, is suspended and will have to sit out the Champions League clash at the Allianz Arena. That is a shame given the way Balotelli broke the resolve of stubborn Everton eight minutes after coming off the bench. The frustration was beginning to boil over as the Toffees parked the bus in front of their goal for the first three-quarters of the game. But Super Mario breathed new life into them and finally cracked the case for a slightly off-colour Manchester City.'

Fellow scorer Milner told how Mario was loved in the City dressing room – and that they did accept he was 'a bit nutty', 'That is pretty accurate. He is a top-quality player though. You have seen those characters around the dressing room. You forget how young he is and he has done a lot in the game already. You can see his quality every time he comes on. He only needed half a chance and he took it. It wasn't an easy finish. He is a massive part of this squad as well. He is a goalscorer. 'He came off the bench and did what you want a substitute to do… make an impact.'

Milner also denied that Balotelli had been moody as he awaited his chance to make a mark at the start of the new season: 'I don't think anyone is happy when they are not in the team. But he hasn't shown it. He trains hard every day. He goes about his business like everyone else does. You try to get in the side and when you get a chance, try to take it. He has not stepped out of line or shown his disappointment in any way.'

Mario was on a roll now: he kept Dzeko out of the side for the next Premier League match, the away match at Blackburn, and scored again as City romped to a 4-0 triumph at Ewood Park. It was just the tonic the club as a whole needed after the demoralising loss at Bayern in the Champions League and the controversy over Carlos Tevez's 'refusal to play' that surrounded it. Mario scored City's second goal at Ewood after latching on to a pass from Samir Nasri and ramming the ball home. It was Mario's third goal in as many games – and he would make it four in four by hitting the back of the net in City's 4-1 demolition of Aston Villa two weeks later.

Significantly, it also signalled the real intent of the club to go all out for the title – after neighbours United had drawn at Liverpool, City now hit the summit of the Premier League. After eight games, City had 22 points – two more than United.

Mario had scored the goal of the match against Villa – a brilliant overhead kick to put his side 1-0 ahead.

It was now all set up nicely for the crunch derby match against United the following week at Old Trafford. This would be the match that would catapult Mario Balotelli into legendary status with City fans as he grabbed a brace in the unforgettable 6-1 thrashing of their biggest rivals. Before the match Mario said he was pleased with his current run of form while pointing out that he had always expected to do well at City – but that he had been held back in his first season because of injury, 'I knew already and Mancini knew how I used to play. Last year I couldn't because of my injury. I couldn't play at the top. But the real Mario is coming now and it isn't the same Mario as last year. Even last year I think I did good because I didn't play for a long time. But this year it's going to be better, I hope. It has to be better. With the injury I wasn't sure about myself or my body. Like with tackles, I didn't do them because I wasn't sure about myself. This year I feel freer.'

He also admitted that he now felt more settled in Manchester and at City, 'This is down to me because it's me that changed my life. Well, I didn't change my life, but things like I don't live in town anymore. I'm outside now so it's quieter. I try to stay at home more. Maybe I'll stay in now with my family, my brother or girlfriend. They weren't here last year, they came sometimes but they were not based here. That's definitely helped. It's quieter now but also I am growing up. If last year I missed home so much, maybe now I miss it a little bit less. I'm OK now, I'm good. I'm happy – the only problem in England is the weather. Everything is getting better.'

And how did he feel about being top of the league with City? He said, 'I was at Inter for four years and I was top of the table. Last year in the Premier League we were second. That was the first time in my life I was second. For me it's normal to be top of the table. That's where I want to be. But we will only stay there if we keep doing the things we are, keep playing like we are.'

The match against United is covered in more detail elsewhere in this book. But it was certainly a turning point for Balotelli at City. The *Telegraph* superbly captured the joy of the blue half of Manchester, saying, 'By the end of the Demolition Derby, Manchester City fans were convulsed with joy, revelling in the sight of the majestic David Silva putting the champions to the sword, serenading Sir Alex Ferguson with "getting sacked in the morning" and designing their "Six and the City" T-shirts. Incredible.' And it was a match Mario said he would 'never forget'; that it would always be in his memory and that he was 'so pleased' for the people who mattered most to him, the brilliant City fans who had backed him through thick and thin since his arrival in Manchester. 'He saw this as a slice of payback to the City fans whom he adores,' I was told. 'Contrary to what many people think – and to the public image the press like to push – he is a man who has a very caring, loyal side to his nature, and who takes criticism deeply. He is much shyer and considerate than his critics make out and he was genuinely thrilled to be part of such a history-making defeat of United – and for the absolute joy he knew it would bring to City fans to thrash United in that way.'

Under the headline, 'Balotelli provides the fireworks as Mancini's side humiliate 10-man hosts to go five points clear', Goal.com also poured scorn on United while lauding City's development, 'Manchester City made a statement that they are no longer just the noisy neighbours but serious title contenders, as a Mario Balotelli double sent his side on the way to a stunning 6-1 win over derby rivals Manchester United.'

And boss Mancini was just as lavish in his praise of Balotelli as the media had been. After the destruction of the Red Devils, Roberto said, 'If we want to talk about Mario the football player we can put him in the first five players in the world. I don't know what happened [over the fireworks incident the previous night at Mario's rented house] apart from he lives in a hotel now. I hope for him and for football that Mario can change his mind. After this, he can become one of the best players in the world like Messi and Ronaldo.

'The problem is because of his age he can make some mistakes. He's Mario.'

Roberto also urged caution to those who were now saying the title was as good as on its way to City. He added, 'I'm satisfied because we beat United away. I don't think there are many teams who can win here. The 6-1 is important for the supporters but I'm just happy for the three points. I think we played very well against Bolton and Tottenham but this is different because we were against a strong team like United. I watched three or four United games from the last month and they conceded a lot of chances to their opponents. I think the season will be very long. There are four or five teams who can win the title. There are 29 games until the end. It's an important win for our confidence and because we showed we are a strong team.'

Mario had now scored six goals in five matches. He was on fire and was showing just why Mancini had such faith in his ability. He was also managing to curb his temper on the field (for the moment at least) – in those five games he had only been booked on one occasion.

More glory and acclaim was on the way – at the start of November 2011, he made his Champions League debut for City and unsurprisingly (given the form he was in) he scored at the end of the first half from the penalty spot after he himself was fouled as the blues went on to crush Spanish outfit Villareal 3-0 away.

It seemed he could do no wrong and Mancini, his team-mates and the fans were all delighted with him. The win moved City into second spot in the tournament's Group A and now they had a real chance to make the next stage along with Bayern Munich, and ahead of Napoli.

A win in Napoli in their next match would see City home and Mancini was brimming with optimism – although he acknowledged they still had a major job to do if they were to win in Italy. He said, 'If we make the knockout stages then anything can happen because we're a good team. We are going very well and want to improve if possible. I enjoyed this performance.

'Villarreal were missing four or five key players but it's still difficult to win away. We had 65 per cent possession and scored three good goals, which is good for confidence. The team have improved in this competition since the first group match. It's always difficult to play in Naples, although we want to win. There will be 70,000 in the stadium, so it will be tough conditions.'

The Sport360.com boys best summed up the night enjoyed by Mario in Villarreal, saying, 'No matter what anyone else does, it's hard to keep Mario Balotelli out of the headlines. Following his heroics in the derby win at Manchester United, the flamboyant frontman marked his Champions League debut for Manchester City with a controversial strike that smoothed their way to success at Villarreal and took them second in Group A.

'Yaya Toure had put Roberto Mancini's men ahead in the 30th minute – the first of his two goals – before Balotelli dealt the Spaniards a decisive blow with a penalty in first-half injury time. He cleverly nutmegged Jose Catala and went down in a sandwich between Gonzalo Rodriguez and Mateo Musacchio with the latter's shove a factor in the spot-kick award.

'Villarreal fumed over a decision they felt was soft but referee Pedro Proenca was unmoved and Balotelli unaffected by suggestions he took a dive. The Italian – back after suspension – waited for keeper Diego Lopez to go to his right and then confidently, almost arrogantly, stroked the ball into the opposite corner.'

After the Villarreal match, Mario spoke to the Press, saying he 'was not mad, but entertaining'. Clearly enjoying his purple spell and basking in the positive publicity, he said, 'I'm not mad as some people say, although sometimes I'm entertaining. I'm ready to take on responsibility, even if people think I'm not. English football is beautiful, wonderful and enjoyable. English football has taught me pressing and chasing back after the opponents when I lose the ball. I don't miss the Italian championship, the standard is very low, while English football is beautiful, wonderful and enjoyable.

His confidence would continue to bring him another goal and more acclaim during the next three weeks as City beat QPR 3-2 away and Newcastle 3-1 at home. Mario scored in the win over the Toon army – and a vital win it was as City emphasised that they were deadly serious about rivalling Man United for the league title. The Toon had arrived in Manchester with their own credentials to be taken as a force in the game; they were on an unbeaten run of 14 league games, breaking a 61-year-old record to achieve that. But City smashed them to bits, at the same time setting down their own marker for a place in the record books. The win meant they had made their own best-ever start to a Premier League campaign and that they had notched up their highest goals scored total for 48 years! Mario scored from the penalty spot and clearly enjoyed his goal and the acclaim from his loyal fans.

He also lapped up the praise of his boss. Mancini purred, It brought lavish praise from boss Mancini, who said later: 'Mario's penalties are fabulous. It's impossible he misses one! I am helping Mario not to waste his talent and become the player he can be – but it is down to him. Today was a really difficult match because Newcastle are a strong team and after the international break it is always difficult. We scored three goals and had other chances but at some moments today we had luck.'

Even Toon boss Alan Pardew admitted that Mario had been a 'handful' to cope with for his suffering centre-halves and added, 'It could have been a different afternoon but it didn't go for us today. We had two good chances at 0-0 and against a team as powerful at City you need a break and we didn't get one. I have no complaints about the penalties but we were doing okay until the first went in.

'The ideas some of the City players present you with and the flair they have makes it difficult for defenders. They are the best team we have played by some distance.'

But just as Balotelli now appeared to be settling down and delivering consistently for City, he went and blew it. As City fan Keith Cooper said, 'Consistency? The only thing consistent about Mario is his inconsistency! He had been on a great run of form and goals for us but then lost it in the next match at Anfield. But the warning signs were there in those previous games – he had been booked in four of the six games before he was sent off at Liverpool.'

That is true. In the game directly prior to the away fixture at Liverpool, Mario had made his first return to his native Italy in a City shirt at Napoli. He handled the inevitable abuse and catcalls from the Napoli supporters and even scored a leveller for City. Indeed the *Sun* commended his behaviour in the face of the antagonism, 'The controversial striker was always going to face a barrage of abuse from the Napoli fans. But he took it all in his stride. He strutted about in his accustomed manner and probably revelled in his role as the pantomime villain – obviously, his reputation went before him. Home fans had the former Inter Milan star marked down as a goalscorer to fear, and he duly obliged with his 33rd-minute equaliser.'

But Mario was frustrated and disappointed with the 2-1 loss at the end of the night – emotions that helped him earn a yellow card. It was his dream to win the Champions League with City – as he had with Inter Milan – and the prospect of playing in the Europa League hardly filled him with joy. But now City were on the brink and would eventually exit the tournament for the dreaded Europa League.

With such a depressing prospect and the jeers of the Napoli crowd still ringing in his ears, Mario headed for the next match, the league clash with Liverpool at Anfield on

Sunday November 27, 2011, in what could be termed 'hardly the best frame of mind'.

Given that situation, Mancini sensibly decided he would start on the bench and brought him on just after the hour with the score at 1-1. He thought Mario had the pace and invention to change the game...well, he was certainly right about Balotelli changing the game, but it was for the worse! Just 18 minutes after his introduction, he was heading for an early bath after two yellows, the first for a foul on Glen Johnson, the second for an elbow on Martin Skrtel. It was his third red since joining City – the others coming against West Brom and Dinamo Kiev – and meant City had to hang on to secure the point that left them five ahead of United at the top of the table.

On his 47th birthday, Mancini was still keen to defend Mario, saying the Liverpool players had helped get him sent off, 'For me the second one was not a yellow card. I don't think that the referee wanted to give a yellow card but the Liverpool players said something. I think the referee gave a free-kick but didn't want to give a yellow until all the Liverpool players complained.

'I watched the replay and, for me, it [the elbow] is nothing. This situation in the Premier League – there are a lot of yellow cards in every game. I don't think all the fouls are yellow cards. Mario should pay attention because he knows many players provoke him and this is not correct.

'We showed strong character because it is very difficult to play here against Liverpool and also because we tried to win, we played well and only in the last 10 minutes we conceded three or four chances but Joe Hart saved well. We conceded two or three chances when we were down to 10 men but we had a good result.'

But then Liverpool manager Kenny Dalglish was critical of Mario, saying, 'I think Balotelli got himself sent off. His actions spoke louder than anybody else's didn't they? Sometimes, if you look in the mirror, you get the answer. Sometimes he doesn't help himself, other times he doesn't get as much leeway as anyone else gets. But, if you help yourself, you don't get in that situation in the first place.'

Mario's red card meant he would sit out the Carling Cup quarter-final win over Arsenal, but that he would be available for the Premier League clash with Norwich.

Mancini chose to have him on the bench for the visit of the Canaries – and warned him in advance that he needed to be cleverer to avoid further dismissals. The boss said, 'Mario should pay attention and he should be clever. I can do nothing - only he is on the pitch. He should pay attention and think only about football. I think he made a mistake only for the first foul when he took the first yellow card. Then he should not take any risks.' Roberto had been particularly disappointed as Mario was on such a hot run of form. He had scored nine times so far that season and was finally living up to his expensive price tag and the potential Mancini continually insisted he had and would eventually realise. Mancini added, 'He is more mature, this is clear. But, in my opinion, if Mario was on the pitch in the last 20 minutes, we could have won the game. It is important Mario understands we need him as a player on the pitch.'

Balotelli was banished to the bench on his return from his ban, but once again showed why Mancini had such belief in him as he came on and scored against Norwich as City stormed to a 5-1 win. This was the match where Mario famously and nonchalantly scored City's fourth goal with his right shoulder, much to the delight of the City fans. American sports writer Eric Freeman brilliantly encapsulated the wonder of the goal and its execution, 'Balotelli took a pass from [Adam] Johnson at the goalmouth, was stonewalled by very British-named Norwich keeper John Ruddy, sought out the rebound right near the goal line, and bumped it in with his right shoulder. It was a cute, arguably insulting way to score, because a more prudent player would have played it in off his head (as if a game that arbitrarily doesn't allow participants to touch the ball with their arms and hands should have a hierarchy of morally upright body parts). The British press and various blogs have responded with the usual round of Balotellian adjectives, adverbs, and phrases: "impishly," "nonchalantly," "outrageous," "again manages to cause a stir," "attention-grabbing," etc.'

Some pundits suggested the goal may have been 'disrespectful' to Norwich, but most football fans – and not just Man City fans – disagreed. One fan said, 'He had the choice between heading it in and doing what he did. He shouldered it in nonchalantly with supreme arrogance and I found it very entertaining. If he'd done that against my team, I think I would have had a minor chuckle (after having a go at him).

'Who cares if it was disrespectful! Fans wind players up and every now and again it's funny to see them show some character and have a go back, in the right way. It was very entertaining and it's only got me loving Balotelli more!'

While a City fan added, 'He gave his answer at Owe Trafford – WHY ALWAYS ME. He is great fun, young and bringing some laughter into the sport after all this racism that is floating around at the moment. It's not as if he was yards away from the goal line, do you think it's disrespectful if a player scores with other legal parts of their body, like using your bum to score? PS I call it Owe Trafford [not Old Trafford] because of the debt [owed] by good family Glazers.'

City coach David Platt couldn't help but smile as he was asked about the goal. Platt said, 'It was a terrific move. But it doesn't matter how you put it in, or whether it's from 12 inches out, it is the same result as a 35-yarder.'

Even then Norwich boss Paul Lambert saluted Mario's confidence, saying, 'Yes, he was very cool and City are a top, top side, their movement was brilliant, they are first class. If you go and play them at their game they will pick you off all over the place. Not many teams will come here and take them on. We kept going, we didn't fold. Our group has a great willingness to try and do well.'

As Christmas 2011 loomed, City were strong favourites to carry on their fine form and romp to their first top-flight league title since 1968. Mario would score his final goal for City in 2011 on Monday December 12, in the 2-1 loss at Chelsea. It was City's first defeat of the season in the Premier League and came after Frank Lampard's goal from the penalty spot. It was not a match they deserved to lose – but it was a warning that they could not afford to take their foot off the pedal if they wanted to take the league title off United in the new year.

They were already out of the Champions League and heading for the Europa League – much to Balotelli's disappointment – and the last thing they wanted to do now was blow up on the domestic front. Mario scored a lovely goal against Chelsea, rounding Petr Cech and slamming the ball home. Mancini said it was the least he could have done – after the boy broke a club 48-hour curfew by visiting a curry house ahead of the match! Football pundit Jamie Redknapp agreed that was probably the case, saying, 'Mario Balotelli is a lucky boy. His manager, Roberto Mancini, clearly rates him and is prepared to overlook some of his antics. It must help they are both Italian and Mancini shows understanding of the emotions of his countryman.

'Before the Manchester derby, fireworks were let off in Balotelli's house and the fire brigade were called. The manager still picked him and he delivered two goals in a 6-1 win. This time, he broke a curfew – and scored after two minutes. A lot of managers would have left him out, but Mancini must say: "You owe me." And Balotelli repays his debts.'

As 2011 turned into 2012 Roberto and all City fans were praying he would continue to repay his debts, and lead them to that elusive promised land of the league title. As always with Mario, it would be a rollercoaster ride. Before we move on to that second half of the 2011/12 campaign, let's examine the conclusion that a number of pundits and fans came to in 2011 – that Mario's actions both on and off the field somewhat mirrored those of another footballing idol who made his name in Manchester a couple of decades earlier.

CHAPTER THIRTEEN

CITY'S CANTONA

Some City fans were none too pleased by the comparison – given that the man with whom he was being categorised was one of rival Manchester United's greatest ever heroes – but I could certainly see why it was made. Why some pundits started to call Balotelli 'the black Cantona' during the 2011/12 season. Mark Ogden, writing in the *Daily Telegraph*, led the way with a brilliant opinion piece, saying, 'Balotelli, the dart-throwing, firework-releasing man-child, has become the modern incarnation of Cantona, despite the motorbike-riding Frenchman's passion for art, acting and Gitanes. For neither cares much for authority or convention. 'Balotelli, as wild as he can be, is a man of the people who will think nothing of offering a £50 tip to the guy who has just cleaned his car or a grateful *Big Issue* vendor on Deansgate. Cantona rejected the Millionaires' Row lifestyle of his United teammates and chose to live in a modest semi-detached house in the Salford suburb of Boothstown.

'And, while their brilliance on a football pitch has ensured adulation and iconic status, both men possess a dark side. Balotelli has been sent off three times in his 18 months at City.'

While Dan Jones, in the *Evening Standard*, described Cantona as a 'a player-aesthete' who operated 'at the point where sport and art intersect: at which the sportsman becomes a performance artist'. He then added, 'Balo combines the devil-may-care combustibility, the self-mythologising, and of course, the glorious talent that was Cantona's hallmark.'

And Jonathan Harwood, in *The Week*, commented, 'Balotelli has some way to go before he matches the exploits of the man who became known as "Le God" in the red half of the city, but he exerts the same kind of fascination as the legendary United number seven. 'Over the last year Balotelli has rarely been out the news. He arrived in England with a bad reputation and was initially seen as a negative influence on his club and the league. But his madcap antics have somehow won over the City faithful and other football fans, and he is now seen as the sort of eccentric always welcome on these shores. His story is not dissimilar to that of Cantona, who moved to England after one too many controversies in France.'

Sun columnist Ian McGarry also pointed out the similarities, saying, when he was watching City at home, 'The talk among the fans was all about Balotelli. And I don't think they were all Manchester City fans either. It occurred to me that this is what it was like when Manchester United had Eric Cantona.'

Even Chelsea main man Didier Drogba got in on the act. Drogba admitted, 'I know Balotelli and he's a nice guy, a funny guy. I like him very much because he's passionate and he loves football. He's a good character for the Premier League, like Cantona, who loves what he is doing. I respect him for that.

'You just have to see what he did in the last few weeks, scoring all those goals for his team, to understand what kind of player he is. I think he knows the league a bit more now, which has made things easier for him too.'

But Cantona himself professed to be unimpressed by the Italian's antics – and rapped Balotelli for his now legendary unveiling of THAT 'Why Always Me?' T-shirt. Cantona said incidents such as his kung fu kick at Crystal Palace were spontaneous – and not pre-planned like Balotelli's T-shirt pose. The Frenchman said, 'I dreamt of being a footballer, of doing great things, of crying and laughing after a victory, of exploding with joy. It is about spontaneity. I never had anything on a T-shirt, never calculated anything. Every action is unique, every reaction unique.'

So is the comparison fair? Well, let's take a closer look...

In one of his most famous comments in 1996 – a year before he quit United - Cantona would say of his time in Manchester, 'I feel close to the rebelliousness and vigour of the youth here. Perhaps time will separate us, but nobody can deny that here, behind the windows of Manchester, there is an insane love of football, of celebration and of music.'

Certainly Balotelli was of the same opinion: he might have felt homesick at times, but he had settled fairly well in the north of England city and even admitted to friends that 'it was pretty similar to Milan'. In its greyness, its rain but also its cultural spark – with music and literature high on the agenda of residents of both cities. And, of course, both Milan and Manchester had two big football teams – Internazionale (Inter Milan) and AC and City and United.

But there were differences between the two men. While, as we have noted, Mario had a troubled upbringing that would mould him as an adult, Eric was settled as a youngster and given the freedom by his parents to develop as a creative being. Cantona was born on May 24 1966 in Marseille in the south of France – his parents named him Eric Daniel Pierre – just two months before England's greatest footballing triumph, when Bobby Moore would lift the World Cup at Wembley. His father's family originated from Sardinia, his mother's from Spain – that production line perhaps helping explain the volatility of his mixed Latin temperament. Yet from an early age Eric was no 'brat'; indeed he much preferred painting and reading in the cave high above the city of Marseille that the family called home.

His father Albert loved painting and hunting. By trade, he was a psychiatric nurse, but he also loved to play football, earning a reputation as a fine amateur goalkeeper. Albert would tell Eric: 'There is nothing more simple than football. Look before you receive the ball and then give it and always remember that the ball goes quicker than you can carry it.'

Eric's mother Eleonore would spend her time bringing up the man who would become known as The King, along with his brothers Jean-Marie and Joel. They were poor, but Eric loved his young life, later claiming he was the 'son of rich people' because of the variety of cultural and artistic activities open to him with his family.

By the age of five he was playing football in the streets and fell in love with the game, saying: 'You start wanting to play [it] when you are three, four or five...you know you have a passion when you can't stop playing the game, when you play it in the streets, in the playground, after school and when you spend your time at school swapping photographs of footballers...playing football in the streets gave us a tremendous need for freedom.'

And like Mario in Italy, Eric certainly had his run-ins on and off the football pitch while in his homeland. His career in France was littered with run-ins with authority and suspensions. By the age of 25, he had quit his homeland and joined Leeds United in February 1992 initially on a loan deal that would see the Yorkshire club pay Nimes £100,000 and Cantona's wages until the end of the season.

Eric would take Leeds to the old First Division championship that season (1991–92) at the expense of Manchester United and his move to Leeds was made permanent, with an extra £1million leaving the Elland Road coffers.

Howard Wilkinson and Eric Cantona? Even in the same sentence the names hardly gel; they grate together, one an English footballing pragmatist and dull, dour Yorkshireman, the other a French romantic, a dreamer, a painter, a poet, a motorcyclist philosopher – a footballer who believed the beautiful game was just that: an opportunity for expression and joyful highs.

It was always going to be a marriage of convenience that would not last, although with Cantona, Sgt Wilko would notch up the one major success of his career.

Wilko remains, to this day, the only Englishman to lead a team to the Premiership title – and it was Leeds' first top-flight in 18 long years. But that was never going to be enough to assuage the demands and ambitions of the King – years later he would say that Leeds, as far as he was concerned, had only been a shop window...a showcase that would ultimately lead to his dream move to the club he was always destined to grace and to lead, Manchester United.

Just as Balotelli found his place at City with his mentor Mancini, so Cantona would now find his 'home' with Ferguson. Legend has it that Fergie signed Cantona as a spur of the moment act. That Leeds MD Bill Fotherby had rang to ask Man United chairman Martin Edwards if Denis Irwin would be available for a move, and that, sitting across from him, Ferguson had scrawled on a piece of paper: 'Ask him if Cantona is for sale'. The piece of paper bit is true, as is the fact that Fotherby rang back later that day to confirm Eric was, indeed, available.

But a source close to Sir Alex told me that Ferguson had been on the case for months. That this was hardly a last-minute move dreamed up from nowhere. That the United manager had been interested when Cantona turned up in England for an initial loan spell at Sheffield Wednesday; that he knew all about the man who had been a nightmare to manage in France.

That he had already earmarked Eric Cantona for a starring role at Old Trafford. That he wanted to pit his managerial skills up against the man who would play the George Best role to his Busby. It would be the ultimate test – and Ferguson was keen to bring it on when Fotherby gave the all-clear.

The wheels had actually been put in motion, I am told, weeks before when then Liverpool boss Gerard Houllier telephoned Ferguson to say that all was not well with Cantona at Leeds and that a bid to Howard Wilkinson might prove fruitful. Fergie bided his time – he did not want to pay over the odds, he knew that Cantona was perceived as the perennial problem boy.

At the end of the day, Wilko was just mighty relieved to get his million quid back.

So it was that on Friday 26 November 1992 Eric Cantona finally came home – for the ridiculously small fee of £1.2million. Of course, Balotelli had cost more than 20 times that amount – but he would tell friends that he too felt relieved to have left Inter Milan to team up with Mancini again. Just as Cantona would rely on Ferguson to provide him with an appropriate stage – and reassurance – to ply his trade, so Balotelli had only ever been able to work with one man...the man who brought him to Eastlands for £22.5million.

But while Cantona would make an immediate impression on his new club, it would take Mario longer to settle – and even longer to prove that he could indeed be the man who could be relied upon and trusted to take City to the very top. Sure, City fans loved him for his unique talent and idiosyncrasies, but they doubted whether he would ever settle enough and knuckle down enough to take them to the very top of the footballing world.

With Cantona, I am told by United insiders that Fergie 'knew immediately that he had struck gold'. That the signing of the Frenchman was the last piece in his jigsaw at the time. Ferguson would later comment on how Cantona had thrilled him by 'walking in as though he owned the bloody place' and that while some players found Old Trafford and the

United aura too much, Cantona was at the very head of the queue of those who 'simply belonged' from day one.

Fergie needed him to settle in quickly if he was to have any hope of winning that first crown for 26 years in 1993 – which he did, and they did. Cantona found at United what he had never experienced before. A club and a manager who embraced and adored him – just as Balotelli did when he arrived at City and was greeted by the man he considers 'the best manager in the world' – his compatriot, Mancini.

And, like Cantona with United, so Mario found with City a club big enough to achieve the major ambitions he himself demanded. A club on the up, with the backing and planned facilities that would conceivably outdo his native Milan clubs in years to come. Cantona found in Ferguson a man who would stand by him and praise him; a manager who knew that the best way to deal with a man like Cantona was with respect and friendship. The big stick had never worked before – so why should it work at Old Trafford? It was the same story with Mancini and Balotelli – Roberto was arguably the only manager in the world who could deal with Mario. He treated him like a surrogate son – and he was certainly the only club manager Balotelli felt totally confident and at ease with.

Cantona arrived in Manchester in November 1992 and soon got to work, showing the kids in the team how it was done and bringing a huge confidence lift to the club. Fergie had joked that United could do with Superman to take them to the next level...well, he didn't get the man of Krypton but the next best thing.

His very own footballing superman – just as Mancini is confident Balotelli will become for City when he has sufficient maturity and commitment, which he believes will come to Mario over the next 12 months. United had been crying out for a superman to lift them from the depths of normality for 26 years. Twenty-six long years since they had last won the league title – just as City were crying out for glory when Balotelli arrived. Within six months of Eric's arrival, the wait that had lasted from 1967 was finally over. The nightmare was over: Cantona was the final piece of the jigsaw, the catalyst for what would become known as The Ferguson Years: two decades of non-stop glory. And for five of them, with Eric in the team, half a decade of non-stop cabaret. Similarly, within his first year at City, Mario had helped them lifted their first major trophy for 35 years. Not only that, he had done so as the official Man of the Match in the clash with Stoke at Wembley.

When Mario arrived at City in 2010, he had walked in with a swagger and a confidence that said, 'Look, I can play...just watch me'. Similarly, Cantona had also walked into Old Trafford like he owned the place: 26 years old, but with more baggage than a normal team might pick up in two lifetimes. He had picked up the tag 'Le Brat' for his adventures in his native France and had managed to fall out with Howard Wilkinson at Leeds within nine months of arriving in the UK.

But it would be his very temperament that would endear him to Manchester United fans – indeed most of us can relate to the rebel, we just usually do not have the guts, or if you look at it another way, the foolhardiness, to act like one. Eric did what he wanted, how he wanted, when he wanted: he remains the ultimate rebel without a pause and earned a permanent place in the heart of United fans.

At Old Trafford, he would forge a partnership with Fergie that would win four Premiership titles in five years, including two league and FA Cup 'doubles' and in 2001 he was voted Manchester United's player of the century. To this day, United fans still refer to him as Eric the King, the Frenchman taking up the mantle that once belonged to the also legendary Denis Law – and this is how the equally loved Bobby Charlton described Eric's qualities in the mid-nineties: 'We're just very grateful he's here. He's such a great player. I'm still pinching myself. A player like that only comes along once or twice in a lifetime, and you don't leave him out or put him in the reserves. You respect his skill. Eric is the brainiest player I've ever seen, he sees such a lot when he has the ball. The big thing he has given United is the ability to make attacks count, not waste good positions until the right option appears, and we now finish almost every move with an effort on goal. The other thing is his ability to release players, even when the pass doesn't look on. If you make the run Eric will probably get you the ball.'

Fergie needed him to settle in quickly if he was to have any hope of winning that first crown for 26 years in 1993. United's season had been a letdown – they were sixth in the table, behind the likes of big-spending Aston Villa and Blackburn Rovers and surprise challengers including Norwich City and QPR.

Goals had been a problem and Fergie prayed that Eric would put that right. Never one for low-level publicity, Eric made his competitive debut as a second-half sub in the derby match against Manchester City at Old Trafford on 12 December 1992. United won 2-1, but Eric was only a bit-part player.

Not a comment you would normally associate with Fergie's Gallic genius, and one that would never again be used.

Eric soon settled down, scoring goals and creating them. His first United goal came in the 1-1 draw at Chelsea on 19 December 1992; his second a week later on Boxing Day as United claimed a point after being 3-0 down at the interval.

The next couple of weeks saw a 5-0 win over Coventry and a 4-1 thrashing of Tottenham – Cantona scored one and made one against Spurs. He had taken United to the top of the table, a slot that would generally be theirs throughout his five years apart from a period during his nine-month ban.

But like Mario, he certainly had that darker side. A side that led to suspensions and bans from the game – disciplinary setbacks that would also hit both their clubs.

The shadow Eric cast over Old Trafford can be seen by the fact that the 1994/95 campaign – which took in the brunt of his ban for the infamous kung fu kick – was the only one of Cantona's five seasons at United in which United failed to win the Premiership, or any other trophy.

As with Mario's indiscretions in Italy, there had been an inkling of the Frenchman's dark side that first season when he spat at a fan on his return to Leeds; an indiscretion that would land him a £1,000 fine from the FA. And, as in 2011 when Balotelli was dropped from the Italian national team because the boss didn't trust him enough, so Cantona was also dropped from the French national team.

But in Cantona's first two seasons at Old Trafford, United went on an amazing run, winning the inaugural Premier League in 1993 by 10 points...and let's not forget they had been six points BEHIND Norwich when Eric walked into Old Trafford. That title breakthrough was vital to Ferguson's ambition of becoming a United great like Sir Matt Busby, but also extra sweet for Eric as it meant he had already wrote himself into English football's history books – by becoming the first player ever to win back-to-back English top-flight titles with different clubs.

Cantona hit nine goals in 22 Premiership games in that first season – and he would lead United to even greater glory in his second, scoring 25 goals in 48 matches and bringing United their first 'double'.

There had even been hopes of a first Treble in the English game – but Aston Villa outplayed the Reds at Wembley in the League Cup final to win 3-1.

But Eric's successful brace of penalties against Chelsea helped United to a comfortable 4-0 triumph in the FA Cup final to secure the 'double'. Then came the icing on the cake – Cantona was named Footballer of the Year by the PFA. In the words of the legendary movie star James Cagney, Eric was certainly 'on top of the world, ma' – and so was his boss. The two were on a winning streak that would seemingly never end – Fergie's gamble on the Frenchman had turned the club around; had turned United back into a major footballing force.

But, just as there was big trouble in Balotelli's second season at City, so would there be big trouble in Eric's third season at Old Trafford. Big, big trouble.

As a boy Cantona had adorned his bedroom wall in the cave above Marseille he called home with pictures of the one and only Bruce Lee. Many years later he would show just how much a hero Lee was to him in an episode that is arguably the most infamous in English football – far beyond anything Mario has ever got up to at City.

Cantona will never be able to shake off that night of kung fu fighting madness at Crystal Palace in January 1995. It was the turning point, the defining moment of his career: his nine-month ban cost United the league and cup, indeed it left them trophy-less at a time when the team was arguably strong enough to win everything; perhaps even the strongest in Ferguson's entire reign at Old Trafford. Yet it did bring an unlikely bonus: for the first time in his career Cantona found a man who would back him when most others were saying, 'Sack him'.

Just as, in March 2012 after City fans had booed Balotelli for arguing on the pitch over a free kick with a team-mate in the 3-3 draw with Sunderland, Mancini had pledged to stand by his man. That, yes, he would stick with Balotelli because he believed he was a genius and that he could turn him around; that he could make him a world beater – another Messi, another Ronaldo.

When Ferguson stuck by Cantona that dark night in 1995, it was also arguably the defining moment of Sir Alex's own managerial career. The boss put his reputation on the line for his mercurial Frenchman and retained Cantona's services. Whereas Sir Matt Busby had struggled and ultimately failed to 'save' Georgie Best from himself, Fergie did save Cantona from imploding. If Eric had left United during the ban for Inter Milan in Italy, who is to say what would have happened to his career?

Would he have knuckled down and changed in the San Siro; would he suddenly have lost the edge that made him the player he was? More likely his indiscretion at Selhurst Park would have been followed by further speedy black marks at Inter – and he might have been cast out of the game for good.

Similarly, if Balotelli had gone back to Milan – and split from his mentor Mancini – his own career could have nosedived as he struggled without Roberto's guidance.

Fergie saved Eric – and his own developing team – by showing him amazing love and loyalty...just as Roberto did with Mario when many pundits and fans were clamouring for him to be sold, to be exiled back to Italy. In Alex Ferguson, Eric finally found the only manager he had ever played under who would hunt him down and plead with him to remain a part of his football club. Similarly, Mario with Mancini – although the Frenchman's indiscretion at Selhurst Park was far more serious than anything Balotelli had ever got up to on a football pitch.

Cantona was sent off at Palace, four minutes into the second half of United's Premiership match there – which ended 1-1 - for kicking out at defender Richard Shaw. As Eric made his way from the pitch, 20-year-old Palace fan Simmons rushed down the stands to taunt him. Cantona was enraged; he responded with his kung fu kick and then exchanged punches with Simmons. As a result, he was banned from football for nine months.

Looking back on the incident there is, of course, no defence for the fact that Cantona finally took his Bruce Lee obsession one kick too far. Sure, Simmons was out of order, but verbal abuse happens all the time in football.

I am assured by one Palace insider that Simmons, a 20-year-old self-employed glazier and 'victim' of Cantona's attack, was not the loyal fan of the club he was usually portrayed. Indeed, I am told his 'first love' was not Palace, but Fulham, and that he returned to Craven Cottage after he was given a life ban from Selhurst for his part in the run-in with Cantona.

Simmons would claim that all he said to Cantona – in true stiff-upper-lip-style English – was along the lines of: 'Off, off, off! Go on, Cantona, that's an early bath for you.' Cantona would say it was a much more racist more along the line of: 'F*** off back to France, you French motherf***er.' Simmons remains adamant that Cantona lied: 'For God's sake you can't say a worse thing about anyone [than what he alleges I said], can you? What he did in saying that was totally unjustified. The man is filth. How can he accuse me of saying such a thing? Where has this allegation against me come from? From him. It ruined my life. And that is why it is inexcusable.'

Simmons would become one of the most recognisable and hated men in Britain: he lost his job, family members ignored him and reporters pursued him.

Most commentators would range against Cantona – describing his assault as 'shameful'. There were a couple of notable dissenters, Jimmy Greaves in the *Sun* and Richard Williams in the *Independent on Sunday*. Greavsie wrote: 'We've heard a lot about Cantona's responsibilities. What about analysing the responsibility of Simmons and every foul-mouthed yob who thinks his £10 admission gives him the right to say what he likes to a man... to abuse, taunt, spit and behave in a way that would get you locked up if you repeated it in the high street.'

And Williams believed that 'Cantona had the excuse of genuine provocation.' He said: 'You didn't have to look very long and hard at Matthew Simmons of Thornton Heath to conclude that Eric Cantona's only mistake was to stop hitting him. The more we discovered about Mr Simmons, the more Cantona's assault looks like the instinctive expression of a flawless moral judgement.'

There was also the belief among United fans that Cantona was being mauled by the British sporting press because he was a foreigner. In a similar way, some people would argue that Balotelli was always on the receiving end of it from the English Press because he was from Italy – maybe another answer to 'Why always me?' question from the man himself.

Certainly, Martin Creasy, a United fanatic since the Seventies, told me he feared it would be the end of Cantona at Old Trafford – and that he believed the Frenchman got a bad deal from the English press precisely because he was from abroad. Creasy said: 'When Eric launched his assault on that Palace moron, I must have been the only United fan still in my seat in stunned disbelief, wondering if this would be the last we would ever see of the greatest United genius since George Best. United fans all around me were too busy jumping up and celebrating Eric's revenge in an incident some in the Press would sneeringly label "The S*** Hits The Fan" to share my immediate concerns. People go on about cutting out racism in football. Total hypocrisy. If Eric had been English, would he have taken the level of crap he did – especially from the Press? Of course not.'

As well as the nine-month ban, Cantona was also sentenced to two weeks in prison which was reduced on appeal to 120 hours community service for the attack. He was also fined £20,000. It was during a news conference after the appeal that he would cryptically refer to the British press as 'a flock of seagulls following the trawler'.

Ferguson's work in travelling to Paris to track down his top player in exile and to persuade him his future was still at Old Trafford was one of the key moves of his time as manager at Old Trafford. Again, there are similarities in how

Mancini refused to give up on Mario when most people – certainly in the Press corps at least – were all for hanging him out to dry. When Mario was sent off at Arsenal in April 2012, most pundits argued he should be sold and the *Sun* even dubbed him 'The man who cost City the title'. Of course, Mario had no more cost the club the title than say Tevez, who had swanned off to play golf in Argentina for half a season, and it didn't cost City the title anyway! And despite initial public misgivings, Roberto would sit down with Mario and talk through how, if he was to stay, he would need to improve his attitude and temperament – he would need to give his all for City.

The duo had many heart-to-hearts in private. Ferguson was much more public in his bid to keep Cantona back then. Indeed, it is the stuff of legend – including how he jumped incognito on the back of a motor cycle for a showdown meeting in a café.

Fergie certainly had a bit of work to do when he arrived in the French capital. It is not always remembered that Cantona actually put in a transfer request in the summer of 1995, the reaction to the news that he had taken part in a practice match against Rochdale. Although it was held behind closed doors at United's training ground, it appeared to breach the terms of the suspension, and the FA opened an inquiry. The boss convinced him all would turn out well if they both stayed solid to their belief in Manchester United.

Richard Williams explained it in this typically elegant way of his: 'By asking for a move, he was making a stand not against the club but against English football. He went off to Paris, apparently intending to talk to the representatives of other clubs. That spring he had received a £4.2m offer from

Massimo Moratti, then recently installed as president of Internazionale. Instead he signed a new contract to stay at Old Trafford, worth £3m over three years. But it was assumed Moratti's offer was on his mind when, in exasperation, he put in his request.

'Sir Alex Ferguson flew to Paris, where he sweet-talked Cantona back to the club. In truth, however, Cantona knew that in England he had found a place where his talent could find its fullest expression. In Italy it would all have been very different. In the Premiership, Cantona's touch and vision shone. In Serie A he would not have stood out to such a degree, if at all. The directness of his play would have gone down well there, but his low boiling point would have betrayed him, perhaps fatally.'

It is an interesting point of view – basically that while Eric was the cream in England he could not cut it in Europe; not only that he could not cut it but also that he knew that. That he stayed for reasons of self-preservation.

What is beyond doubt is that Ferguson definitely made that summer trip to France in 1995 out of self-preservation – and admiration for the man who was on the brink of implosion. Sir Alex was naturally upset and bewildered by the events of that crazy night. He would admit that he had not seen the incident – and that it only dawned on him when he watched the video of it over and over again when he got back home to Manchester at 4am the following morning.

It was a Burns Night the proud Scot would never forget. Many years later Fergie would later admit that what he saw on the video was 'pretty appalling' and say: 'Over the years since then I have never been able to elicit an explanation of the episode from Eric, but my own feeling is that anger at himself over the ordering-off and resentment of the referee's earlier inaction [at the way Palace players were getting away with fouling him] combined to take him over the brink.'

But he never had the slightest doubt that he and United should move Heaven and earth to keep the Frenchman. Just as Mancini remained convinced in his belief that Mario should be kept at City, not just because he would become good – but because he would become one of the three best players in the world…along with Lionel Messi and Cristiano Ronaldo and, yes, better than Rooney!

Cantona was Ferguson's talisman; the man who had made the difference – now it was payback time, time to stand by the footballer extraordinaire who had made Fergie's dream come true. His efforts would pay dividends: Eric would serve his ban and stay at United for almost another two years. Eric would later admit that his love of United and the fans had played a key role in his decision to stay, saying: 'I feel close to the rebelliousness and vigour of the youth here. Perhaps time will separate us, but nobody can deny that here, behind the windows of Manchester there is an insane love of football, of celebration and of music.'

The United boss was in no doubt that he had done right to fight for Cantona – he needed only look at how United suffered badly as a consequence of the fall-out from that traumatic night to see that. At the start of 1995 things had been looking good for Ferguson. He had just been awarded the CBE in the New Year honours list; he had bought Andy Cole for £7million from Newcastle United and United looked on their way to a third Premier League title.

But the Red Devils would lose the plot after January 25 and failure to win at West Ham on the last day of the season and falling to Everton in the FA Cup Final meant that the trophy cabinet at Old Trafford was empty for the first time in five years.

Ferguson would grind his teeth on the Cantona Speaks video and complain: 'I think it's summed up in the three games we had in a row at home (between March 15 and April 17). We drew 0-0 with Chelsea, 0-0 with Tottenham and 0-0 with Leeds United. Having only lost the League by one point, no one's going to tell me or even attempt to convince me that he would not have made one goal or scored a goal in one of those three games.'

But Cantona would soon be back at the top table.

Mario's 'seagulls' moment would come with the 'Why always me' poser on his T-shirt that time – although it was, of course, in no way as cryptic as the Frenchman's comment! Just like Cantona, Mario has always stressed how determined he was to be a success on the European stage. 'Playing in the Champions League is of key importance to him,' I am told. 'Mario wants to play against the best – and win against the best. That was one of the reasons why he agreed to move to City and work with Mancini. He believed Roberto could lead City to the Champions League given the resources he had to work with from the wealthy owners.'

Certainly, disillusionment with United's inability to crack the Champions League at the time led to Cantona quitting United in 1997. He had won four league titles in five years with United, but admitted he had lost his love for the game. He was particularly anguished to have failed yet again in Europe – United were eliminated by Borussia Dortmund in the semi-finals of the Champions League, and felt that he had become a marketing tool at Old Trafford.

In his 1999 autobiography *Managing My Life*, Sir Alex said that Eric told him of his decision to retire within 24 hours of United's European exit – confirming how badly the legendary Frenchman had taken the defeat.

But it would be another month before he left for good, his last competitive game being the 2-0 home win over West Ham on May 11, 1997.

Cantona would later explain his exit from football in this way: 'When you quit football it is not easy, your life becomes difficult. I should know because sometimes I feel I quit too young. I loved the game but I no longer had the passion to go to bed early, not to go out with my friends, not to drink, and not to do a lot of other things – the things I like in life.'

Cantona had scored a total of 82 goals in 185 appearances for United in five marvellous years. Fergie knew he would be missed...and would miss him, his professionalism, his genius and the way he inspired those around him.

United legend Mark Hughes would later sum up the unique relationship between the boss and his star player in this way in his autobiography, Hughsie: 'Alex Ferguson didn't exactly rewrite the rule book but he treated him differently and explained to the rest of us that he was a special player requiring special treatment.'

It rings a bell when you think of Mancini and Balotelli. In the 2011-12 season Roberto defiantly stood by Mario when the boy was on the end of a constant barrage of criticism from the Press – particularly after the 3-3 draw with Sunderland. The *Daily Mail* summed up the mood in Fleet Street regarding Balotelli, 'Manchester City manager Roberto Mancini will not give up on maverick striker Mario Balotelli. The mercurial forward remains a source of recurring frustration for Mancini but the City boss still wants to coax the best out of him. Mancini was highly critical of the 21-year-old's overall display in Saturday's clash with Sunderland despite his two goals in the 3-3 draw at the Etihad Stadium.' But when asked whether he would give up on Mario, Mancini said, 'No. I am frustrated because sometimes I think it is not possible that a player with his class and his technique can play a game like this. I think he is young and I hope for him he can improve very quickly for his future. A player like Mario in the Premier League should score one or two goals every game.' It could have been Ferguson talking about Cantona 17 years earlier. Now let's fast forward to 2012 and look at Mario's contribution to that wonderful title win for City.

CHAPTER FOURTEEN

JUST CHAMPION

There's a school of thought among some football commentators that in 2012 Manchester City won their first top-flight title since 1968 despite Mario Balotelli – rather than because of him.

They say that it was only after he was sent off at Arsenal on April 12, 2012, that City finally caught fire again, throwing off their shackles and stomping to a brilliant title win when many had written them off.

But my own feeling is that Mario is being treated pretty harshly with that assessment. I know fellow pundits would mutter, 'Well, you would say that, wouldn't you – seeing as you are writing a book about him'. But the facts alone suggest Balotelli played an important role in that first title win since 1968. In the first half of the season, he scored key goals and helped City to the top of the table. His tally from September to December 2011 was 11 goals in 14 appearances – a rate which most strikers would kill for.

Then, at the very end of the campaign, wasn't he the very man who set up the last-gasp goal for Aguero to score and settle the title race? Yes, in the very last game of the season – with City drawing 2-2 at home to Queens Park Rangers and the title heading to rivals United who had won 1-0 at Sunderland – Mario had come on as a sub and stabbed the ball across to the Spanish goal king who duly dispatched the ball home and sent the blue side of Manchester into ecstasy.

If Mario hadn't have been in the right place at the right time, City would have drawn – and United would have been celebrating their 20th top-flight title win. So don't give me that line that Balotelli played no part in ensuring the crown ended up at City.

Sure, I'm not denying that the second half of the season was in many ways a disappointment for Balotelli – that his indiscipline and sulking meant he let himself and the team down. His problems in 2012 began towards the end of January when he came on as a 65th-minute substitute for Edin Dzeko in the 3-2 home win over Tottenham.

The match showed both the best and the worst of Balotelli. Not long after his appearance he was booked for a foul on Benoit Assou-Ekotto and then appeared to take a massive – and nasty – gamble by stamping on Scott Parker as the England midfielder lay on the ground.

The incident was not seen by referee Howard Webb and so Mario avoided a certain red card. But he would ultimately suffer for his act of madness when the FA reviewed the incident and charged him with violent conduct for the kick against Parker. Mario would subsequently be suspended for four matches, three for violent conduct and one for his second sending off.

Yet in the same match he would be the City hero – keeping remarkable cool and poise to score from the penalty spot in injury time after he himself was fouled in the box by Ledley King. This would lead to his now famous 'Cantona pose' as he stretched his body back and stared proudly ahead, chin in the air. Certainly many pundits and fans would nod sagely in agreement when it was suggested that City had found their own version of United's enfant terrible – as we also have already suggested and examined in this book.

That injury time winner would add to his legend with City fans – and add to the resentment felt by their Spurs counter-parts who insisted he shouldn't even have been on the pitch to score it after his stamp on Parker.

And then Spurs boss Harry Redknapp was certainly of the opinion that Mario should have had an early bath. 'He should have gone,' Redknapp said. 'He's backheeled him straight in the head. It is not the first time he has done that and I am sure it won't be the last. I am the last person to talk about getting people sent off and what they should and shouldn't do. But it is blatant. He reacts to challenges like that at times. Scott has got a cut on his head.

'It is up to their manager to deal with it. I have got my own opinions but I don't like people kicking other people in the head on football pitches. I don't think it's wrong to say that. Why you should backheel someone in the head when they are lying on the floor is beyond me. It's not a nice thing to do.'

City coach David Platt said: 'I never saw anything live and there was nothing from the players live either. Until we have seen it we cannot really comment. What we are aware of from the last month is that different TV angles can show different things.'

It would be Platt who would react to the news that Mario would be banned for four games – assuming City accepted the decision. If they appealed, it could be more. Platt added that it seemed unfair Mario would be judged by going back to look at the video of the incident again – if it was done in one high-profile case, shouldn't all the Premier League matches be examined for similar incidents?

Platt said, 'We are likely to be without Mario for four games. We found out the information last night – but it seems inconsistent. I have seen it from an angle where I can think the referee saw it live, like I did. Other people saw it live and didn't react, nobody, not one of the Tottenham players or staff. The referee didn't react live. It is when you slow it down that all the reactions come.

'I don't know what has gone on but there seems a huge inconsistency in refereeing matches on a Monday morning. Shouldn't you revisit everything that has happened over the weekend?'

The ban meant Mario would now miss the Carling Cup semi-final second leg return at Liverpool plus league games against Everton, Fulham and Aston Villa.

When he did return to league action, he proved his worth to the team by scoring in the 3-0 win over Blackburn at the Etihad on February 25. Mario also found the back of the net in the 2–0 home win against Bolton and the 3-2 home win in the Europa League over Sporting Lisbon (although it would not be enough to stop the Blues exiting the tournament on the away goals rule).

But it was a nine-day period at the end of March and the start of April 2012 that would prove the most damaging of Mario's time at City – a period of time that would even leave boss Mancini exasperated. On March 31, Mario scored twice as City drew 3–3 at home to Sunderland. But he was seen by millions on TV arguing and jostling with full-back Aleksandar Kolarov over who should take a free kick. That left Mancini enraged – and the City boss would later admit he had even contemplated substituting Mario after 5 minutes of the 90.

Mancini did not sound at all grateful that his fellow countryman had at least saved a point for City with those two goals (a first half penalty and a late second). He said, 'I thought about taking Mario off after five minutes but in the end he scored two goals. He didn't play well. In a game like this the strikers should be the difference - but not in the last two minutes, in the minutes before. A player like Mario or [Edin] Dzeko should score two or three goals in a game like this. In this moment we need Carlos Tevez, a striker who can do different. I want this.'

The loss of two points against the Black Cats meant United were now top of the table with 73 points, followed by City on 71 – and the worry now for Mancini was that United would soon ease five points clear by beating Blackburn Rovers at Ewood Park. Mancini added optimistically, 'I think United will probably draw and we will be three points behind. It is hard but we have another seven games. We have done some mistakes in the last games but also United can arrive in a difficult moment. It is important we are there.'

To the neutral it looked as if the title race was over – that City had lost their nerve and that United would now romp home given their experience in the end-of-season run-ins accumulated over the years. That view was firmed up when United did beat Blackburn, moving five points clear.

It was surely as good as over? Certainly City travelled to Arsenal on 8 April more in hope than expectation for a match they could not afford to lose. They did, 1-0 – and Mario was blamed from all quarters after getting sent off, for the third time that season, and dubbed 'The man who lost City the title' by the tabloids.

A goal by Mikel Arteta, three minutes from time, looked to have ended City's dream and the thousands of fans who had made the journey to the capital now trudged despondently back to their coaches, convinced the title had been lost. Balotelli had been sent off for a second yellow card after a poor tackle on Gunners full-back Bacary Sagna. He had also lunged at Alex Song and the pundits claimed he would now been banned for nine matches. The Mail explained how the speculation had come about, 'Mario Balotelli is facing a nine-game 'totting up' ban after the FA revealed they are deciding whether to punish his studs-up tackle on Arsenal's Alex Song, which referee Martin Atkinson missed. If they do, it would count as a fourth red card of the season for the Italian.

'Balotelli was sent off anyway late in the defeat by Arsenal for a second yellow card. He already misses one game for that sending off and an extra two because it was his third red of the season. He has been shown two reds on the pitch, plus another retrospective ban for his stamp on Tottenham's Scott Parker. He could be banned for a further three games for the Song tackle and then for another three because that would count as his fourth red.'

Surely Balotelli had run out of time and chances at the Etihad?

After the match Mancini said, 'Mario should have been sent off after 20 minutes. I've finished my words for him. I've finished. I love him as a guy, as a player. I know him. He's not a bad guy and is a fantastic player. But, at this moment, I'm very sorry for him because he continues to lose his talent, his quality.

'I hope, for him, he can understand that he's in a bad way for his future. And he can change his behaviour in the future. But I'm finished. We have six games left and he will not play. It's not sure he'll [be available] because he could get a three- or four-game ban. Now, I need to be sure that I have always 11 players on the pitch. With Mario, it's always a big risk. Every time we risk one [man] being sent off, even if he can also score in the last minute.'

Asked if he would now sell him, Mancini said: 'Probably' and then added, 'I am disappointed in him. He is young and he continues to make a lot of mistakes. I have punished him during the season – it's totally false that I have different behaviour with Mario than the other players – and he still needs to change his behaviour if he wants to improve. I've seen players with huge talent finish in two or three years because they do not change. I hope, for him, he will.'

It sounded like a sad epitaph for Balotelli's City career and he was understandably down as the team made their way back to Manchester. 'He's not a bad lad,' a source told me, 'he just needs to learn to control his short fuse…you don't want him to lose his edge, but he has got to learn. That night he was like a frightened young boy – it seemed as if he was at the end of the road at City and that made him sad and scared. He loved the fans and knew he had let them down. He apologised to Mancini and the team and just prayed that somehow he would come out of the other side with one final chance.'

Somehow he would do just that. It was probably down to the fact that he was only banned for three games (not the nine as some had predicted) and, remarkably, given that he seemed to be at the point of no-return after the Arsenal game, would even play again that season.

City had only one of their last six away games and were 8 points behind United with 6 games to go. It looked an impossible chasm to clear – although there was still a chink of light, as Mancini pointed out, 'Now the title is more difficult, but we have 18 points to play for and a derby at home. United have had an incredible run in the last two months. But, in football, it can change. Ten days ago we were one point behind. Today it's eight points. United have more experience than us, so probably it's difficult, but until it's impossible, we keep going.'

Well, City certainly did keep going, reducing the gap by beating United at home and then seeing United drop points unexpectedly – so that by the final day of the season the fate of the title battle was, remarkably, back in the hands of Mancini's men.

From being eight points behind, they knew on Sunday May 13 that they would win the league – irrelevant of how United fared at Sunderland – if they beat QPR at home. The *Sun* summed up how ironic it was that City won the game and the title in time added on, 'Manchester City won the greatest Premier League title race in history – and they did it in Fergie time. City scored twice in the final two minutes of added time to beat QPR and lift their first title since 1968.'

Aguero was mobbed after his winning goal – but he pointed at Balotelli to thank him for setting it up and the Italian was finally forgiven for his misdeeds by the City players and their fans. It was a true *Roy of the Rovers*-style ending to a season that had looked like ending in heartache for City and Mario, with the latter looking a certainty to be sold after his sending off at Arsenal.

Mario Balotelli had earned redemption with that final flick-on to Aguero – he had played a final role in City winning the title, and no one could argue with that.

Afterwards City fans revelled in watching Mancini celebrate and then seeing images of Ferguson and his United team in bits. So many times Fergie had won on nail-biting, last-gasp occasions like this – now he was finally tasting his own medicine, and the City fans felt no guilt at all as they celebrated his misery.

After the match Mancini said: 'After this I feel 90 years old. It's incredible, you cannot think of a final game like this – that would be impossible. It was a crazy end to a crazy season. I think it's incredible for me and all our supporters. I'm very happy for them, the season is for them – all our supporters. When we were losing it was a terrible feeling, then in a moment it was simply incredible. I have never experienced anything like this in my whole career.'

While Ferguson said: 'We knew five minutes of extra time was being played at City. Our game had three minutes of stoppage time. You don't know what can happen in the extra two minutes but they got that break and won the game. It is a cruel way to have the title ripped away but I've had a lot of ups and downs in my 25 years here.'

Mancini wasn't done yet. 'We deserved this and I am very proud of my players,' he added. 'They fought to the end because they all wanted this title so much. I think for us it was really important to win this championship, now Manchester City can have a big future. We have changed the history of this football club.'

Match-winner Aguero scored in the 94th minute and promptly burst into tears! He was quick to praise Balotelli for being selfless. Aguero said, 'I thought Mario Balotelli was going to have a go himself but he just moved it on one more and it fell at my feet. My only thought was to hit the target and it went in. For sure it was the most important goal of my career. You score a goal in the last minute to win the title – I'm not sure that is ever going to happen again.

'QPR were fighting for their lives. They sat back and we knew they would make things difficult for us on the counter-attack. During the pitch invasion, loads of fans came over. They grabbed me and kissed me. But the only thing I understood was "I love you". That made me so happy. Since I arrived at City, everyone has treated me really well. I repaid them with a goal to win the title and make history.'

So the last word on the triumph was left, appropriately, to Balotelli, the man who had so redeemed himself at the 11th hour. Mario said: 'We are the best and that's why we won. We didn't play very well in a few games but for the rest of the season we played very well, so we deserved to win. Personally I think too many people talked and too many people said bad things about me. Now they have just to shut up.

'Manchester City is a great club, a great team, I have great team-mates. I don't see my future far from here so I think I want to be here.'

That was some end to his second season at City – and one that now ensured he would be at the Etihad at the start of the 2012/13 campaign. But while many of his team-mates now ventured off for a richly deserved summer break, Mario Balotelli headed off to Poland and the Ukraine with the Italy squad, determined to carry on his late burst of fine form and enthusiasm at Euro 2012. It would be a further sign of his development that, by the end of the tournament, he would be widely recognised as the best No 9 taking part.

But the journey from his teenage years to international acclaim with Italy was a long, sometimes torturous one. Mario's international career with Italy did not take off as quickly as he would have hoped. He would certainly have been selected and played for the Italian national under-15 and under-17 teams – but was not eligible as he did not obtain Italian citizenship until he was aged 18. Up until that time, he was still seen as a Ghanaian immigrant. The situation arose because his natural parents refused to allow the Balotellis to officially adopt him. His foster mother Silvia Balotelli explained in 2006 what that meant in real terms, 'Every two years I have to go to the local police station to renew the residence permit of Mario. After hours in line, I hand over the ticket and then take away a piece of paper. It's as if he arrived in Italy only yesterday. A boy born in Italy and entrusted to an Italian family for 15 years is considered as an immigrant. Mario, like all Italian boys, would like to visit Europe, to do an English course in England like his classmates – but he cannot.'

Five days before his 17th birthday in 2007, Ghana tried to take advantage of the situation by offering Mario the chance to play for them. He was called up to that country's senior squad by head coach Claude Le Roy for a friendly against Senegal in London – but refused the offer, saying he wanted to play for Italy when he finally got his Italian passport.

Finally, when he hit the age of 18 he was granted Italian citizenship and was now available to play for the country closest to his heart. He scored on his Under-21 debut in the 1-1 draw with Greece in September, 2008, but controversy was never far away and he showed his good and bad side in the 2009 Euro Under-21 Championship. Typically, Mario scored against Sweden but was then dismissed before the interval for an altercation with one of the Swedish youngsters.

Italy went on to win 2-1 and a suitably chastened Mario apologised to his team-mates and said, 'The referee was already angry before I made that challenge, so I knew straight after that a red card would be shown. The team had to play with ten men from there, but luckily they did fantastic, so I must praise my brave comrades for their efforts today.' In total, Mario made 16 appearances for the Italian under-21s and scored six goals.

He would go on to make his debut for the senior team just days before he signed for Manchester City. It would not be a debut to remember as Italy slumped to a shock 1-0 defeat against the Ivory Coast in a match played at Upton Park, West Ham. Mario had said beforehand that he was determined to be a winner with Italy – and said he was disappointed not to have hit the back of the net in five previous appearances, 'I need to wake up and get going,' he said. 'For me scoring is the biggest thing. Victories are important but so are goals. I know I can arrive to the top. If I'm good up front it's not because I'm fortunate.'

Soon he would score that elusive first senior international goal. It would arrive on 11 November, 2011, in the 2–0 win in Poland and it would earn him a place in the history books...as the first black player to score for the Italian national team.

Fast forward seven months and Mario would become the first black player to represent Italy at a major tournament - when he started their 1-1 draw with Spain on June 10. This would be the tournament that would propel him to worldwide fame and acclaim – he would prove he did have the skill and ability to become, as Mancini had predicted two years earlier, one of the best footballers in the world.

In the second match, Mario would become the first black player to score for Italy in a tournament – as they beat Ireland 2-0. His goal came in the last minute, and it was a belter as he volleyed home from a late corner, leaving the Irish defence for dead. After scoring he seemed to mouth some words at coach Cesare Prandelli – allegedly because Prandelli had left him out of the starting line-up. He was stopped in his tracks by his good friend and team-mate Leonardo Bonucci, who threw his hand around Balotelli's mouth.

The goal helped Italy to the quarter-finals and they then, of course, disposed of England. It ended 0-0 after 120 minutes but the Italians won 4-2 on penalties. Mario scored the first penalty, calmly beating Joe Hart in the shootout, his confidence oozing forth and leading the way for his team-mates to follow suit.

But it was in the next match, the semi-final against the Germans that Balotelli truly showed his class and that he deserved to play on the biggest world stages. It was arguably the best display of his career as he destroyed the German machine with two wonderful goals.

The Germans had been the pre-tournament favourites of many to win the trophy, but they fell well short as Balotelli tormented them with a swashbuckling display at No 9, scoring his first goal with a powerful header and his second with a magnificent piledriver that gave Manuel Neuer no chance in the German goal.

Mario had come of age and both head coaches knew he had been the difference. Italy boss Prandelli said: "Mario was excellent, like the entire team. He ran into space and was always available. He was focused and did exactly what I asked of him,' while his German counterpart Joachim Low admitted that Balotelli had been 'a handful' and 'difficult to contain'.

After scoring his second goal, Mario had whipped off his shirt and stood defiantly with his fists clenched and his eyes staring, unmoving. I was told that this was his reply to those in his homeland who still could not see him as a footballer; those who still saw him as a black person first and then a footballer. In particular, it was apparently a riposte to the unforgivable cartoon in Italy's daily newspaper *Gazzetta dello Sport*, which had printed a cartoon portraying him as King Kong.

It was bad timing: Mario had been fighting for years against racist attitudes in the Italian game and had made it clear before Euro 2012 that he would 'kill' anyone who threw a banana at him in the street and that he would walk off the pitch if he heard racist chanting at the tournament.

Afterwards Mario spoke about that goal celebration, saying, 'There is nothing really to say about my celebration for my second goal. You saw it. You can judge. Did somebody get angry with the jubilation of the second goal? Because they saw my body and they are jealous. Anyway, I don't have a special celebration for the final. I just hope I score. I think about scoring – I don't think about a celebration.'

The Italian media were keen for him to return home now that he was becoming an international superstar, but he made it clear he would not be leaving City. No, he loved the fans at the Etihad far too much to do that, 'Come back now? No, I go back to Manchester. The City fans always want me, even though they are British – and I have helped eliminate their national team. It's been a special year for me. We won the Premier League at Manchester City last season – so having a good season doesn't depend on me winning the Euros. Yes, it would be something special for me but if we don't win it, it wouldn't spoil the other things.'

Mario ran to his foster mother Silvia behind the goal and was embraced by her after the match. He said, Balotelli added: 'I am really happy and, on Sunday, I hope I will be even more happy. We are in the final. We are one of the two best teams in the tournament, so we have to go there and play to win. I went to my mum and I said, "These goals are for you". It was the most beautiful night of my life but I hope that this Sunday is even better. The final is for my dad – and

I hope to make it four goals in this tournament. If we win and I score, it will be amazing. But if I don't score and we win, it will still be amazing.'

Italy boss Cesare Prandelli also praised the meteoric development of his star striker, saying of Mario, 'He has enormous potential. He has a good coach in Mancini, who will help him grow. Mario now wants to repeat his performance against Germany on Sunday.'

In the event, Mario was not able to repeat his performance against Spain in the final as Italy crashed 4-0. Starved of service, he worked hard but, like his team-mates, was unable to deny the brilliant Spanish their deserved moment of glory.

At the end of a demoralising encounter – which saw a 10-man Italy forced to defend against Spain after using all their substitutes and losing one of them to injury – Mario stormed down the tunnel at full-time, pushing past an Italian FA official on his way. He re-emerged, in tears, to collect his runners-up medal, but was still distraught as he and his team-mates made their way off the pitch.

Coach Prandelli offered words of comfort to his star striker and afterwards told the Press, 'I told Mario that these are experiences you have to deal with and have to accept. You also have to make sure this helps you going forward and you can grow from the experience. This has happened to a number of players, and will happen again, but this is what sport is all about.'

It was the end of a dramatic year of football for the Manchester City striker, who had now become the most talked-about footballer on the planet. In the next, and final, chapter we will look at some of those stories that put Mario on the front, as well as the back, pages of newspapers around the world – and decide which are fact and which are fiction.

CHAPTER FIFTEEN

FACT AND FICTION

'There's only one player that is a little stronger than me: Messi. All of the others are behind me.'

Mario Balotelli, 2011

Of course Mario is as famed for his antics away from the game as he is for his feats on the field. Never far away from a front page splash as he is from one on the back pages of the tabloids, he is a red-top hack's dream – whether a news reporter or a football writer. Not since the halcyon days of David Beckham has a footballer dominated the newspaper execs' agenda as Mario now does in England.

His every move – and mistake – is documented in print and online. There is no hiding place and so any unfavourable incident can cause particular problems and run-ins with his boss at City, Roberto Mancini.

In this chapter, we will try to get our heads around some

of the numerous incidents Mario has allegedly been involved in (others are covered in separate chapters on Inter Milan and Mario's first two seasons at City) and try to make sense of whether they are inventions of the media and the gossip-makers, or have some truth in them. Plus we will look at some items from people close to Mario and Manchester City that have NOT been bandied about in public, but which are said to hold some authenticity.

All the anecdotes are in no particular chronological order – neither are they rated in order of perceived importance. Just days before he arrived at City in August, 2010, Mario had to make a public apology after he and a group of friends fired air pistols in the open in Milan's Piazza della Repubblica. 'I did a stupid thing when I fired the pistol,' he told Sky Sports after he played 59 minutes in Italy's 1-0 loss to Ivory Coast. 'But the journalists blew everything out of proportion. And it's not true that I'm not a team player.'

That statement appeared hard to justify at an earlier match for the Italian national team when he angered the manager by refusing to wear the new home kit endorsed by the Italian FA. Balotelli came out in the old kit, claiming he didn't like the new one...

And then there was the incident in Italy in October 2010 when Mario and his 17-year-old brother Enoch drove into a women's prison in their hometown of Brescia. They had been curious to see just what it was like – and apparently wandered around for a few minutes before they were detained and questioned by prison officers. Italian newspaper *Gazzetta dello Sport* claimed the duo were eventually released after half an hour of questioning. Prison officer Calogero Lo Presti told the paper, 'It was 1600 when we saw a high-powered Mercedes come through the gate. Inside were two boys, after a few minutes we realised one of them was Balotelli. Physically we recognised him, but that is not enough, so we proceeded with official procedure. At the end they both appeared a bit frightened.

'They said they saw the gate opened and never imagined they would need a special permit to visit the prison. The two were particularly intrigued by the fact it was a women's prison. Balotelli has apologised. He spoke in a low voice, he was a little embarrassed.' Balotelli's agent, Mino Raiola, played down the incident and said, 'Mario has done nothing wrong. Indeed, the officers have praised him for his initiative. Certainly they explained this could have been avoided, but it ended there. What I find strange is that a public official rushed to say what had happened. Nothing happened. It was only emphasised because it's Mario.'

Mario was a City player at the time – he had returned home for a few days' break. The hacks in England were fascinated by his antics away from the pitch and devoted acres of newsprint to him as he now returned to City. The *Daily Mail*, for instance, did a piece on Mario and his 'extravagant lifestyle' – the standfirst of which sums up how the tabloids quickly viewed the man they have dubbed, 'Madcap Mario'. It read like this, 'He's the Manchester City footballer who this week admitted to having a fling with the same prostitute as Wayne Rooney. This is the same star who, last year, caused a blaze at his £3m Cheshire mansion by shooting fireworks out of the bathroom window with his friends. The 21-year-old, who is paid £125,000-a-week, has collected an estimated £10,000 worth of parking tickets leaving his Bentley on double yellow lines. His home is a seven-bedroom mansion reached by a sweeping drive, at the end of which an ornate stone fountain surrounded by a circular miniature box hedge creates a turning circle for visitors' cars – not to mention his own, a white £140,000 Bentley Continental GT with a top speed of 198mph.

'The £3million house is familiar to Cheshire firemen who, late last year, were called there at 1am and had to use breathing apparatus while putting out a fierce blaze on the first floor started by fireworks being shot out of the bathroom window.'

Yes...the infamous fireworks incident. It happened on Saturday October 21, 2011, when Mario had a few friends around for the evening at 'the £3million house in Cheshire' (which he was only renting by the way). Yes, a firework was set off in the bathroom and, yes, the fire brigade were needed to put out a blaze in the bathroom that was threatening to spread elsewhere. The *Sun* reported the incident thus, 'Two fire engines were sent to the house of Mario Balotelli last night – after a firework went off in his bathroom. The Manchester City striker escaped unharmed after the late night incident at his home. Cheshire Fire and Rescue Service discovered a fire in the bathroom on the first floor, with four firefighters dousing the flames using their hose. A spokesman for the fire department said: "Crews managed to put the fire out within half an hour of arriving but remained at the scene until 2.45am to prevent any possible flare-ups. Smoke alarms were fitted at the property and the occupiers were able to get out unharmed. The fire was caused by a firework."'

But, contrary to most reports, I am assured that Mario was NOT involved in setting off the fireworks and was therefore certainly NOT to blame for the blaze. It was the act of one of his guests, who certainly was out of order and 'probably a little tipsy'. The guest apparently – and dangerously – was trying to throw the firework out of the bathroom window towards some other revellers who were enjoying a drink in the back garden of the house.

Mario's culpability began and ended with the fact that he had invited guests who would even contemplate letting off a firework in a house, and for not keeping an eye on them. Regarding the latter, I am told that he had gone to bed an hour or so before the incident, that he was keen to get some shut-eye before a certain football match the following day that just happened to be against arch rivals, Manchester United.

Of course, Mancini was not happy about the incident or the headlines – and neither were the club – but they accepted Balotelli's explanation of events. He told them he was 'really angry' with his friend and the aggravation that followed, which cost him more than just his beauty sleep. He apparently had to cough up the best part of £100,000 to sort out the wrecked bathroom suite and rid the house of smoke damage at the property in Mottram St Andrew, a leafy Cheshire suburb.

On top of that, he ran up a bill approaching another £50k staying in a £1,000 a night suite at the Hilton Hotel in Manchester city centre until he could return to the Cheshire house after it was refurbished. But all City fans cared about the following day in October 2011 was how he would perform against United at Old Trafford in the Premier League clash. He certainly did not let them down – scoring two of the goals as they thrashed United 6-1.

It was United's worst home defeat since February 1955 and

meant that City went five points clear at the top of the Premier League. As a statement of intent from City and Balotelli, it was of the highest order. Forget the fireworks off the pitch; Mario had put United to the sword on it. City fans revelled in United's misery and that of Sir Alex Ferguson, who had admitted, 'It's the worst result in my history. The impact will come from the embarrassment of the defeat. I can't believe the scoreline. Even as a player I don't think I ever lost 6-1. That's a challenge for me too.'

Then there are the stories of Mario and his car(s). Perhaps the most famous from his time in Manchester involves the estimated £10,000-worth of parking tickets he has collected by leaving his Bentley and Maserati on double yellow lines. True or false? True apparently. If Mario sees an outfit he likes in a shop, or fancies a cappuccino, he gets it there and then, and sorts out the bills for the tickets later.

And there's the tale of what happened two weeks after Mario had arrived at City and crashed his Audi R8 near the club's Carrington training ground. Police were quickly on the scene to breathalyse, question and search the young Italian. They then found 15 grand in notes in the Bentley's glove compartment. Suspicious as to its origins, they grilled him and asked him how he had got the money and why he was carrying it. 'I am rich,' he told them with a smile. They let him go on his merry way, shaking their heads. True or false? Again, true according to sources.

Back in Italy, Mario was accused of glamorising the Mafia because he visited one of the most notorious strongholds of the Camorra, the criminal organisation based in Naples. The Italian newspaper *La Stampa* accused him of wandering the rough area 'as though it were Disney World'. It was alleged that Mario was given an escorted tour by two Camorra godfathers. The information emerged from a leaked anti-mafia police report, but Mario vehemently denied the claims, saying he was simply visiting and was unaware of the identities of anyone he met there.

Mario said, 'I really didn't know who these people were. That day in Naples there were loads of people milling around me in the street.'

Mario's agent Mino Raiola said he had gone on the tour 'to satisfy his curiosity' and added, 'All that I know for sure is that Balotelli has never had any kind of ties with organised crime. Certainly he didn't know that the people he was with were connected to the mob.'

Italian police accepted that version of events and confirmed that Mario was not suspected of any wrongdoing.

After the furore, Mario then wrote an open letter to the Italian press explaining in more detail what happened on that trip – and why it happened and denying all the claims made against him. It was not picked up by the British Press (maybe because they prefer the bad news about the boy rather than the good?) but here is a transcript, from Italian to English, in Mario's own words: 'Around a year ago I was invited to Naples to pick up the Golden Boy award and stopped for a few days on vacation. I was taken to see many wonderful places in Naples, like Piazza del Plebiscito, but I also asked to visit those areas off the beaten track. Having seen the film Gomorra, I was amazed by this whole other reality that exists.

'I wanted to see for myself and understand the serious problems in the suburbs of Naples that the film talked about. It is a very different reality to the one I grew up with and experience now. Some prefer to turn their heads and pretend nothing is happening, but I am not like that. When I went to Brazil in 2008 I asked to visit the favelas and poorest quarters of Bahia so I could meet and talk to people, then play football in the streets with the local kids.

'In Naples one morning I visited the Quartieri Spagnoli area, where I remember playing football with the children in the street, then crossed the Scampia quarter. After a while I asked to leave, because I realised it was a dangerous situation. I did not know that police were investigating or watching me that day, nor was I ever called to testify.

'Frankly, I don't understand how a statement from a "confidential informer" could be handed to the newspapers. Only in Italy can this sort of thing happen. I am profoundly disgusted by the fact my actions in good faith were used against me in this way. I realise I am naive, but linking my name to the betting scandal as well is absolutely too much. I have nothing to do with betting, let alone organised crime.

'I am absolutely calm and invite the police to do all the investigating they need, because I have nothing to hide. I have sent my lawyers to punish those who want to use my name and suggest I'm involved in anything illegal.

'Finally, I think at this delicate moment for Italian football we don't need further controversy, but rather focus on resolving the real problems.'

Mario himself has denied some of the stories circulating about him. He told Oasis rocker and City fanatic Noel Gallagher that the following two tales had no substance:

After winning £25,000 in a casino, Balotelli handed a homeless man £1,000 in cash. When asked why, he said it was because he liked his ginger dreadlocks and beard. 'Not true,' he confirmed to Noel. And he also denied that he has taken a young lad into school and spoken to the headmaster about him after the boy had turned up at the City training ground. The boy had allegedly told Mario that he was being bullied at the school. Mario admitted that he had spoken to a boy about being absent from school at Carrington – but had NOT taken him to school and chatted to the headmaster.

And Mario denied that he came back with just a quad bike after his mother had sent him to John Lewis for an ironing board – no, he came back with a quad bike AND a trampoline! He also apparently turned the landscaped gardens at his rented house into a dirt track upon which he could ride the quad bike to his heart's content!

But it is untrue that on Christmas Eve 2011 that he walked into the Tudor pub at Peel Hall, a Grade II country house near his Cheshire home, and astonished customers by producing £1,000 in cash from his pocket to put behind the bar to treat everybody. And that he later put another grand into the collecting plate after Midnight Mass at the local church – although I am informed he DID go to the church and put £200 on the plate, still a generous offering.

Mario further denies that he ever went into a petrol station in Manchester and paid for everyone's fuel.

But he did once invite home a magician he met in Manchester's Trafford Centre – and asked the bemused guy to teach him some tricks. The magician duly did just that but Mario found it difficult to get the hang of them.

Another two apparently correct anecdotes concern darts and fans. In the first, he was pulled up and bollocked by Mancini after he had thrown darts at members of the Man

City youth team. He said he did it because, 'I got bored and wanted to pass some time.'

And after City's devastating 6-1 win at United, he drove through Manchester city centre and high-fived City fans out of his car window.

It was during that win, of course, that the legend of Balotelli was firmly embellished when he scored and revealed a T-shirt underneath his blue City top, emblazoned with the now legendary words, 'Why always me?' Asked if he had prepared the message because he thought he would score – and because he was disenchanted with his treatment at City, Mario replied, 'I thought I was going to score three. The T-shirt was just a message. It's not a question that people do to me, it's a question that I do to them. It was to all the people that talk bad about me and say stuff not nice and they don't know me so [I was] asking: 'Why always me, like, why always me?''

I was told there are more instances of Mario's madcap antics away from the club. For instance, one day he apparently found a stray cat at the Carrington training centre and took it home to his rented house to care for it. All fine you might say, but the tenancy was said to emphasise that no animals were allowed in the house.

Then there is the tale of how he once wandered into a library in Manchester and liked it so much that he asked if he could pay off the fines of everyone in the city who owed money on overdue books.

On the field of play, there was the case of the night in Kiev – when Mario did not appear for the second half of a Europa League game after suffering an allergic reaction to the grass. Some pundits claimed that he had stayed in the dressing